Анатолий Лядов   Anatoly Lyadov
(1855–1914)

ПОЛНОЕ
СОБРАНИЕ СОЧИНЕНИЙ

Complete Works · Sämtliche Werke
Œuvres complètes

для фортепиано
for piano · für Klavier · pour piano

IV

Urtext

Редакция · Edited by · Herausgegeben von · Edité par
Victor Yekimovsky
Nikolay Tolstoi
K 305
Könemann Music Budapest

INDEX

Две фуги op. 41 5
Deux Fugues

Две прелюдии и мазурка op. 42 12
Deux Préludes et Mazurka

Мазурка 16
Mazurka

Баркарола op. 44 19
Barcarolle

Четыре прелюдии op. 46 24
Quatre Préludes

Этюд и канцонетта op. 48 30
Étude et Canzonetta

Вариации на польскую народную песню op. 51 38
Variations sur un thème populaire polonais

Три балетных номера op. 52 54
Trois Morceaux de ballet

Три багатели op. 53 64
Trois Bagatelles

Три пьесы op. 57
Trois Morceaux

    1. Прелюдия 68
        Prélude
    2. Вальс 70
        Valse
    3. Мазурка 73
        Mazurka

Четыре пьесы op. 64
Quatre Morceaux

    1. Гримаса 74
        Grimace – Grimasse – Grimace
    2. Сумрак 74
        Twilight – Halbdunkel – Ténébres
    3. Искушение 76
        Temptation – Versuchung – Tentation
    4. Воспоминание 78
        Reminiscence – Erinnerung – Réminiscence

APPENDIX

Шествие (1889) 79
The Procession

Прелюдия-пастораль (1894) 81
Prélude-pastorale

Сарабанда (1895) 83
Sarabande

Прелюдия (1897) 84
Prélude

Вариации на русскую тему (1899) 85
Variations sur un thème russe

Танец комара (1911) 88
Dance of the Mosquito – Mückentanz – Danse de Moustique

Фуга на тему Ля – До – Фа (1913) 89
Fugue on the Theme "La – Do – Fa"

12 канонов на один cantus firmus (1914) 90
12 canons on a cantus firmus

Notes 92

Две фуги   Deux Fugues

Посвящается Герману Августовичу Ларошу

Op.41.
1896

Allegro moderato ♩=88

p legato

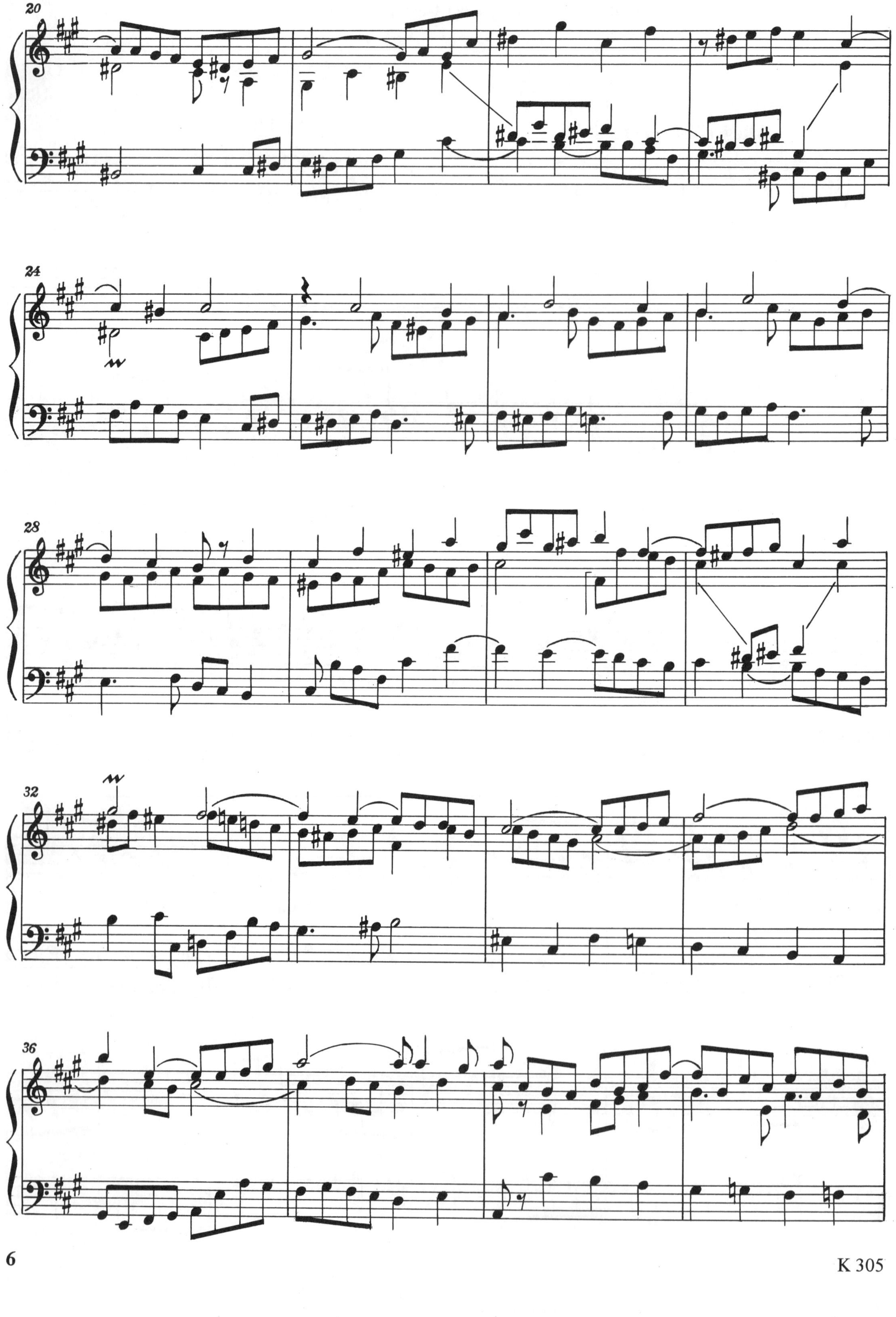
20
24
28
32
36

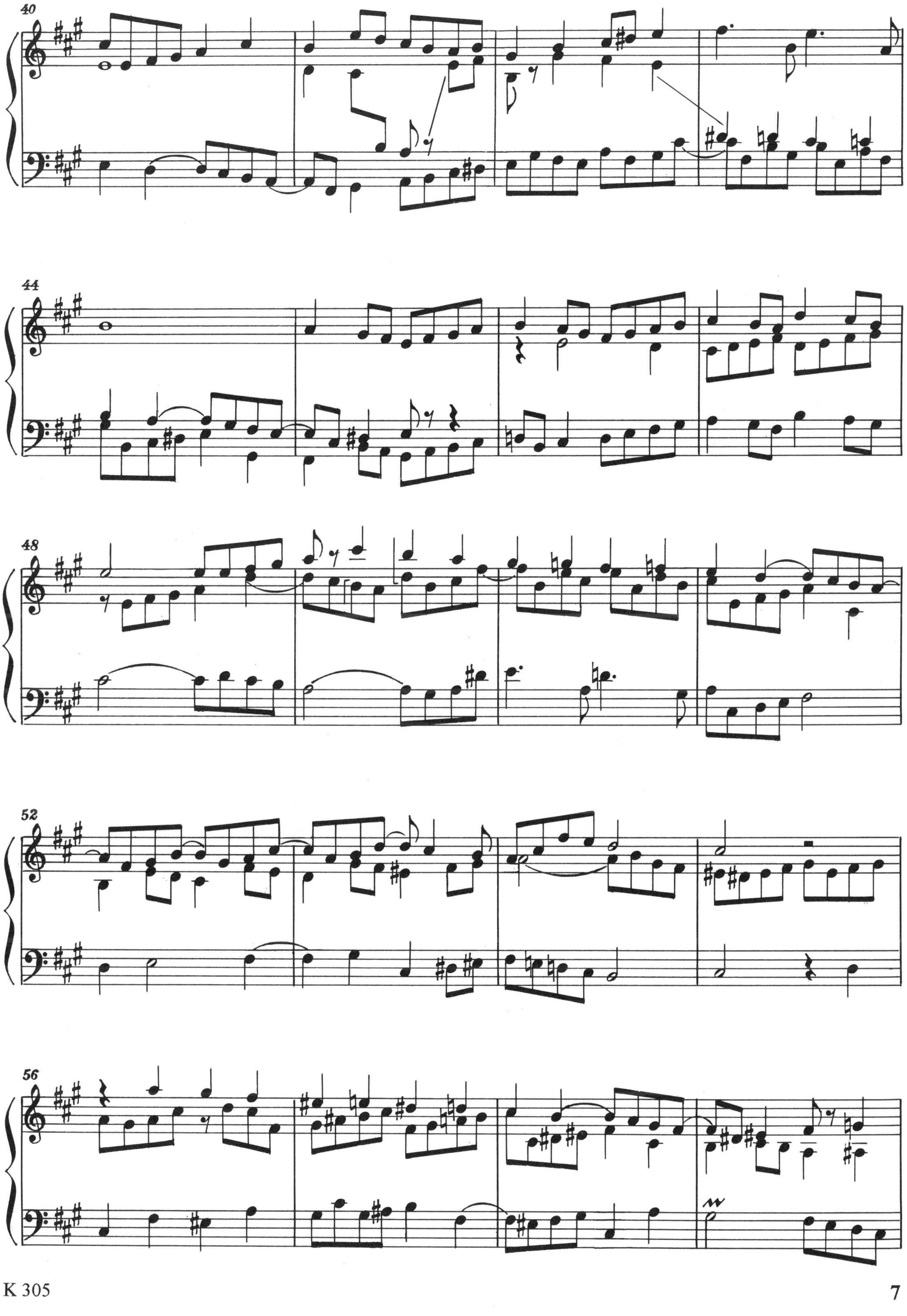
40
44
48
52
56

Полыновка, 7-го июня 1896 г.

Allegretto ♩=84

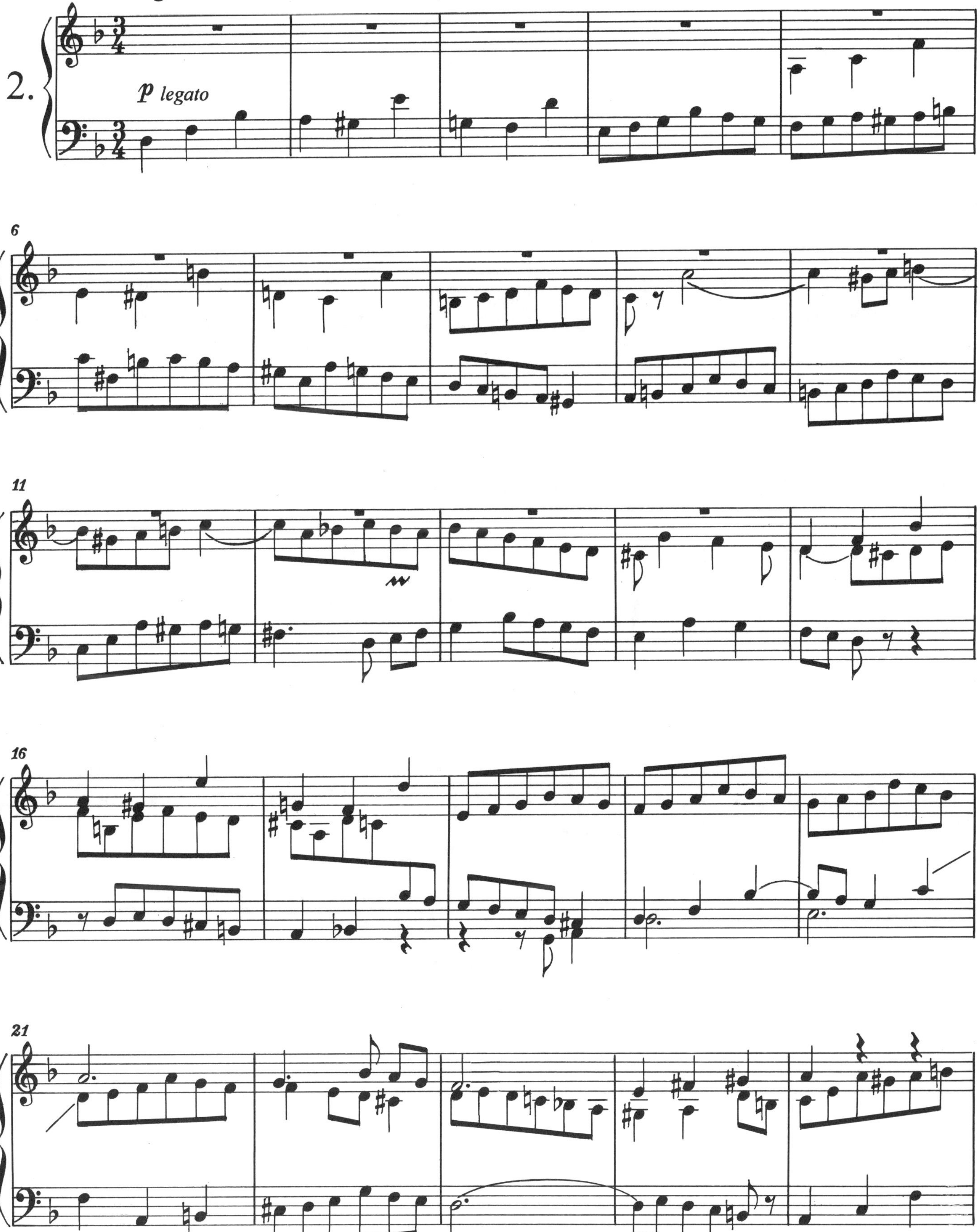

K 305

Полыновка, 15-го июня 1896 г.

ДВЕ ПРЕЛЮДИИ И МАЗУРКА
DEUX PRÉLUDES ET MAZURKA

Посвящается Шульц-Эвлеру

Op.42.
1898

Прелюдия   Prélude

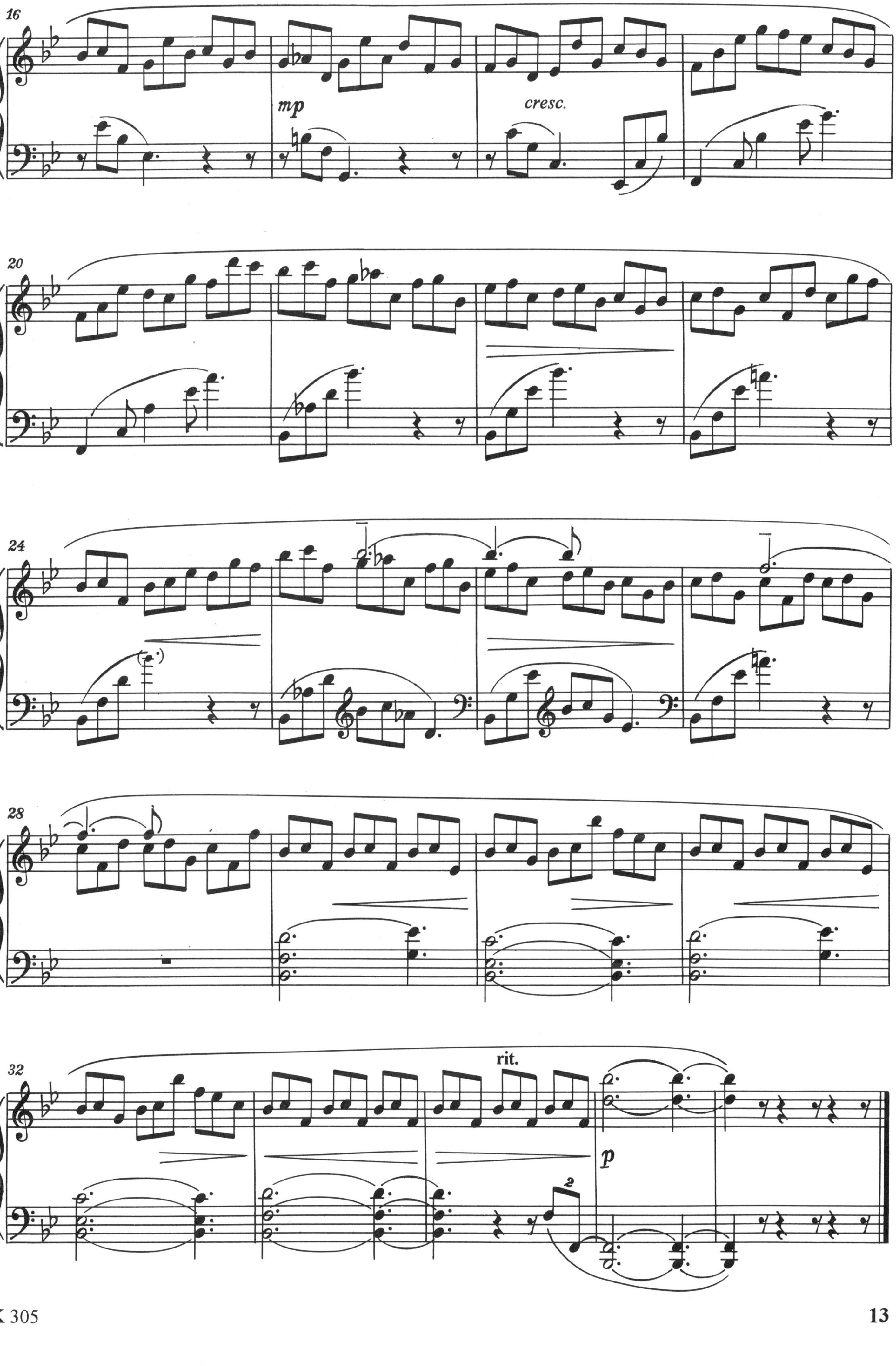
16
mp
cresc.
20
24
28
32
rit.
p

Прелюдия   Prélude

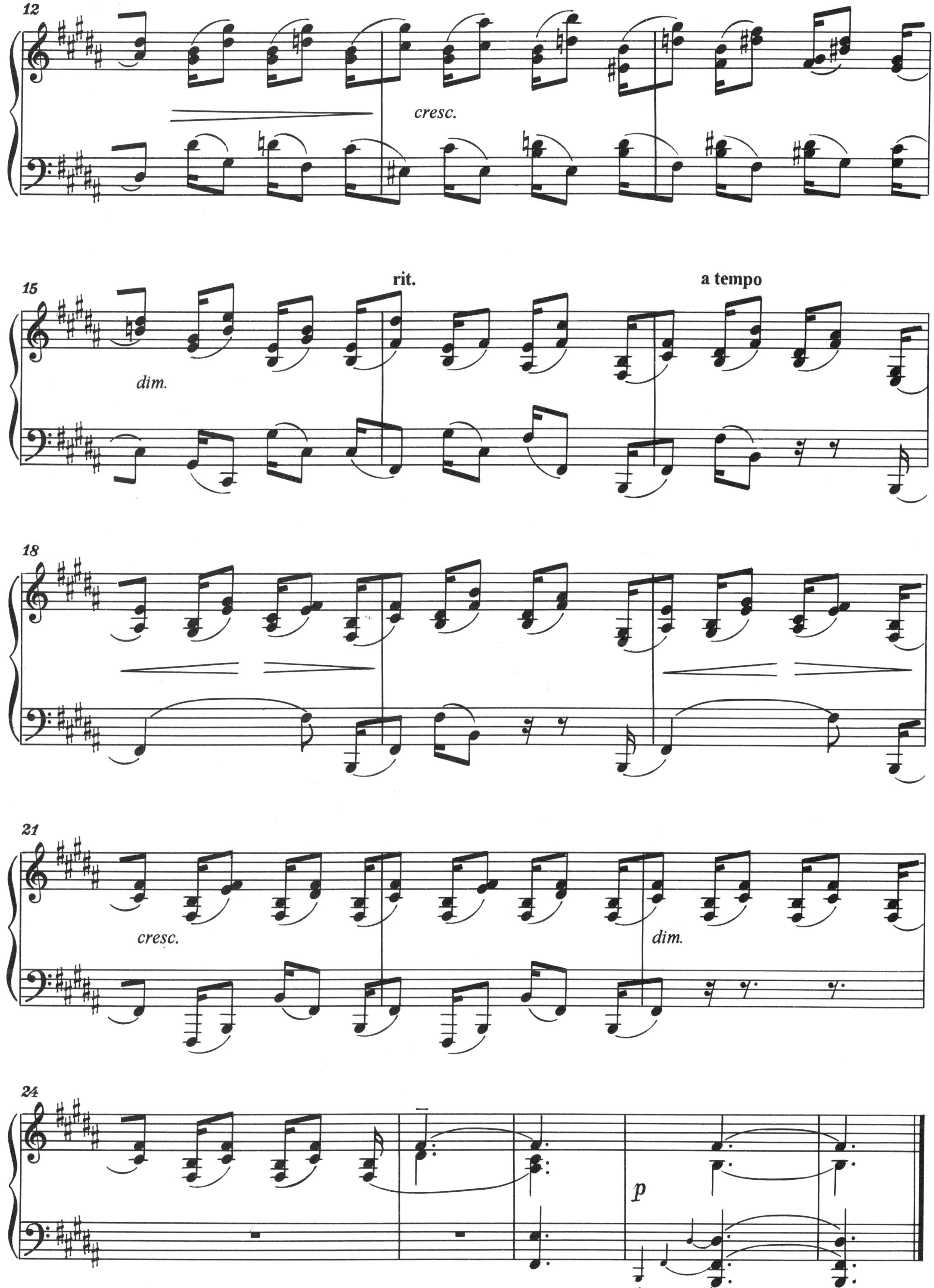
12
cresc.
15
rit.
a tempo
dim.
18
21
cresc.
dim.
24
p

Мазурка
на польские темы

Mazurka
sur thèmes polonaises

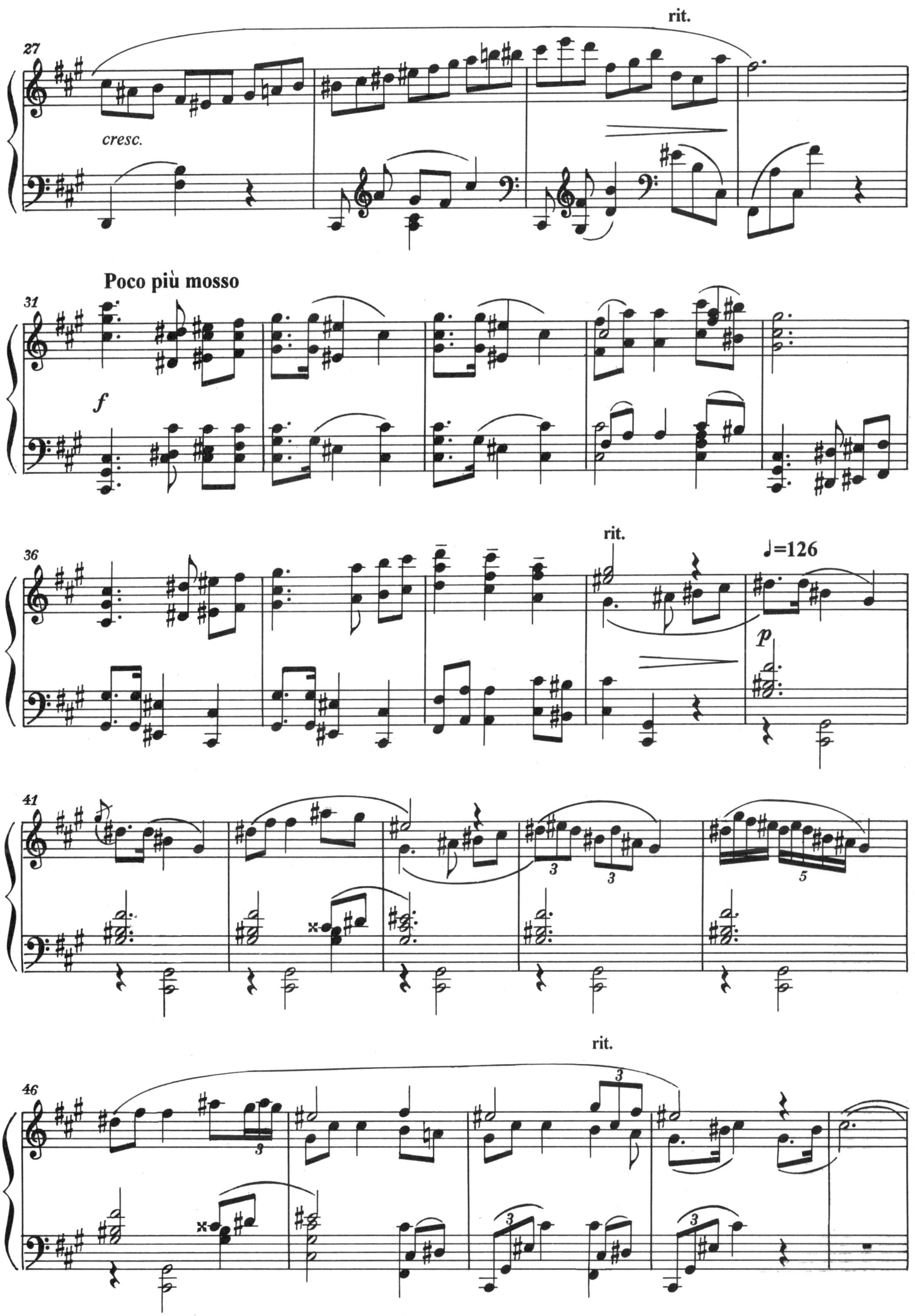
rit.
cresc.
Poco più mosso
f
rit.
♩=126
p
rit.

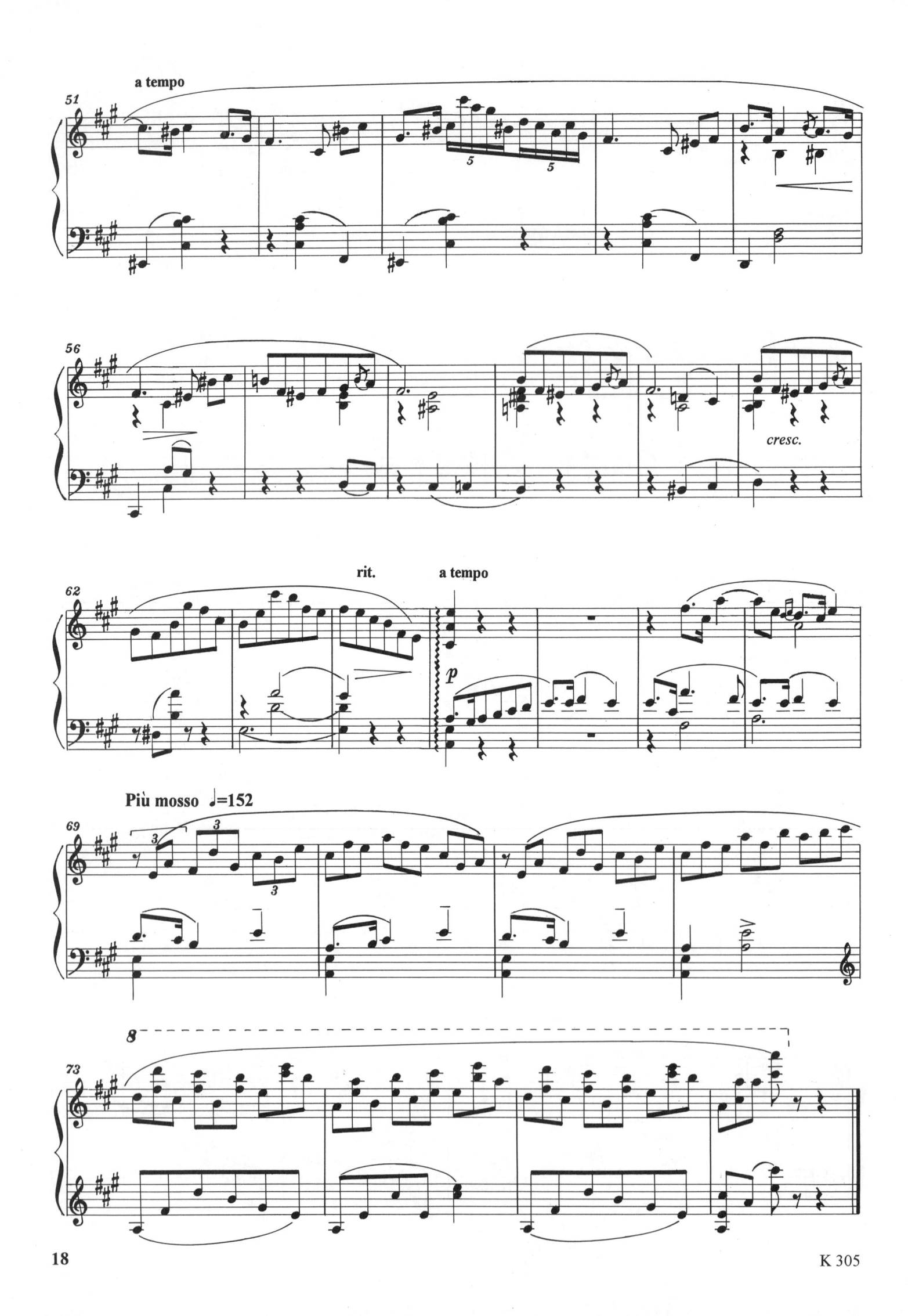
a tempo
51
56
cresc.
62
rit.
a tempo
p
Più mosso ♩=152
69
73

Баркарола / Barcarolle

Посвящается Варваре Семеновне Ревковской

Op.44.
1898

Andante amorevale ♩=96

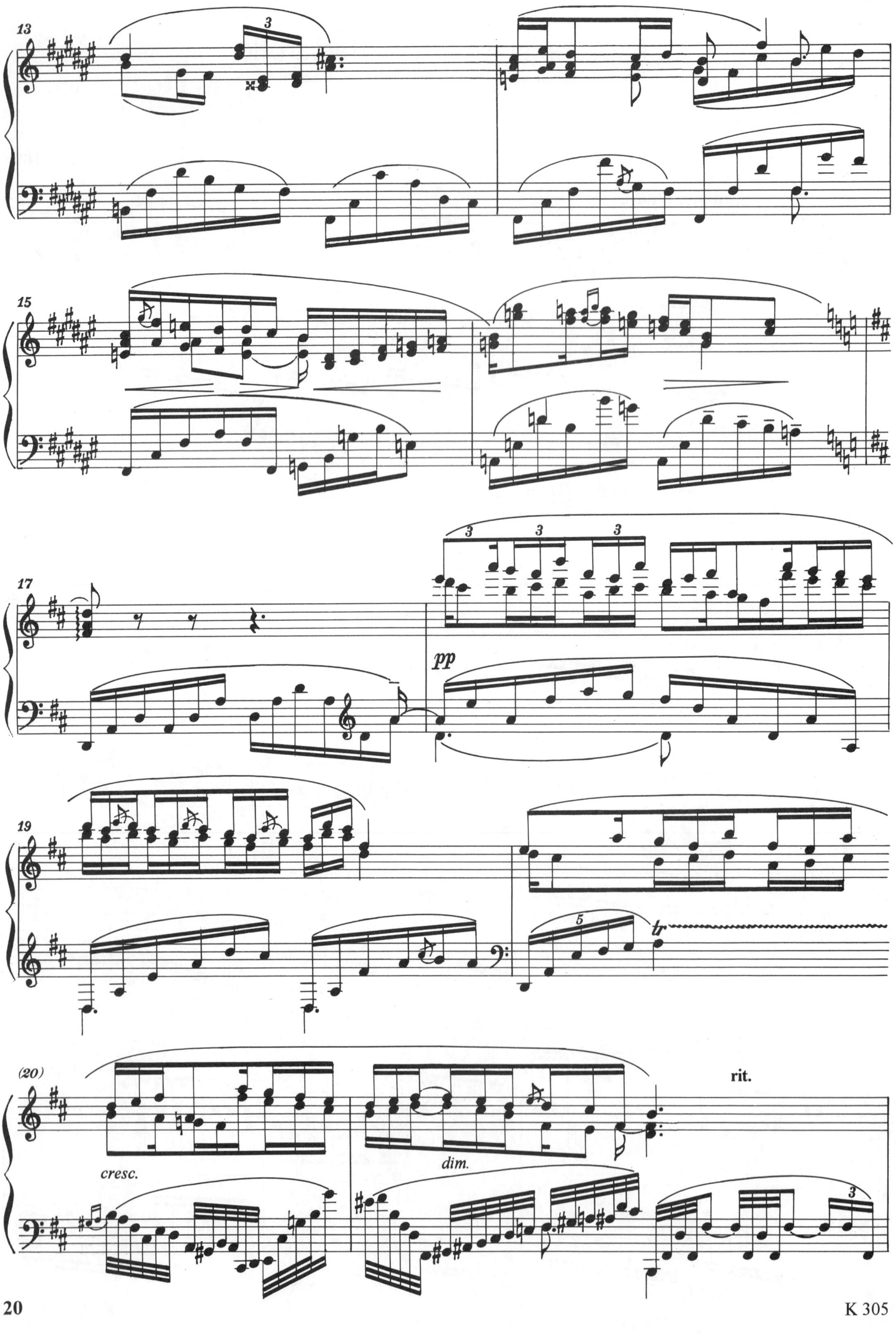
13
3
15
17
3
3
3
pp
19
5
tr
(20)
rit.
cresc.
dim.
3

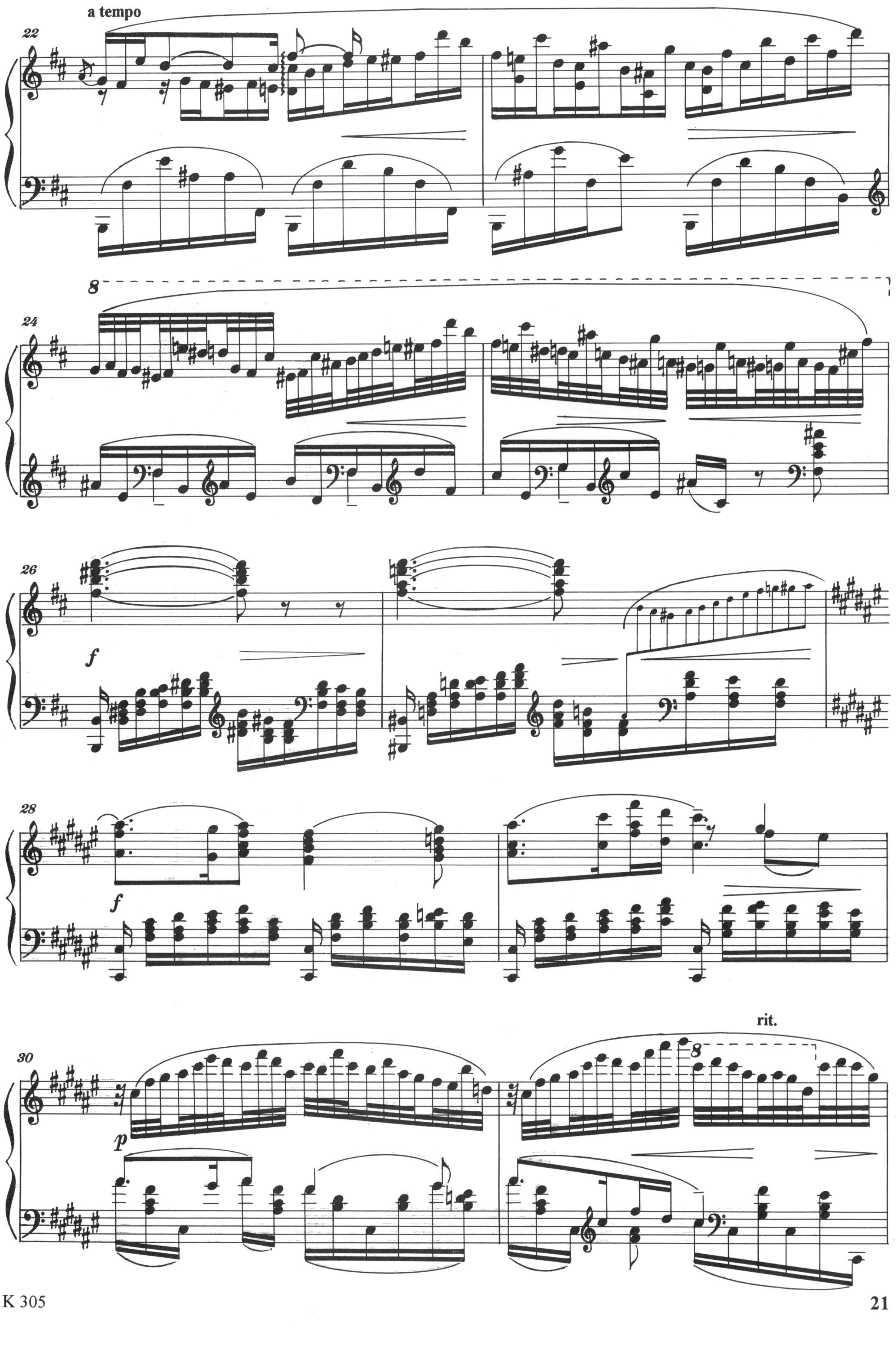
a tempo
22
24
8
26
f
28
f
30
p
rit.
8

Più mosso
32
mf
cresc.
35
f
38
cresc.
ff p
cresc.
41
3
3
3
cresc.
44
dim.

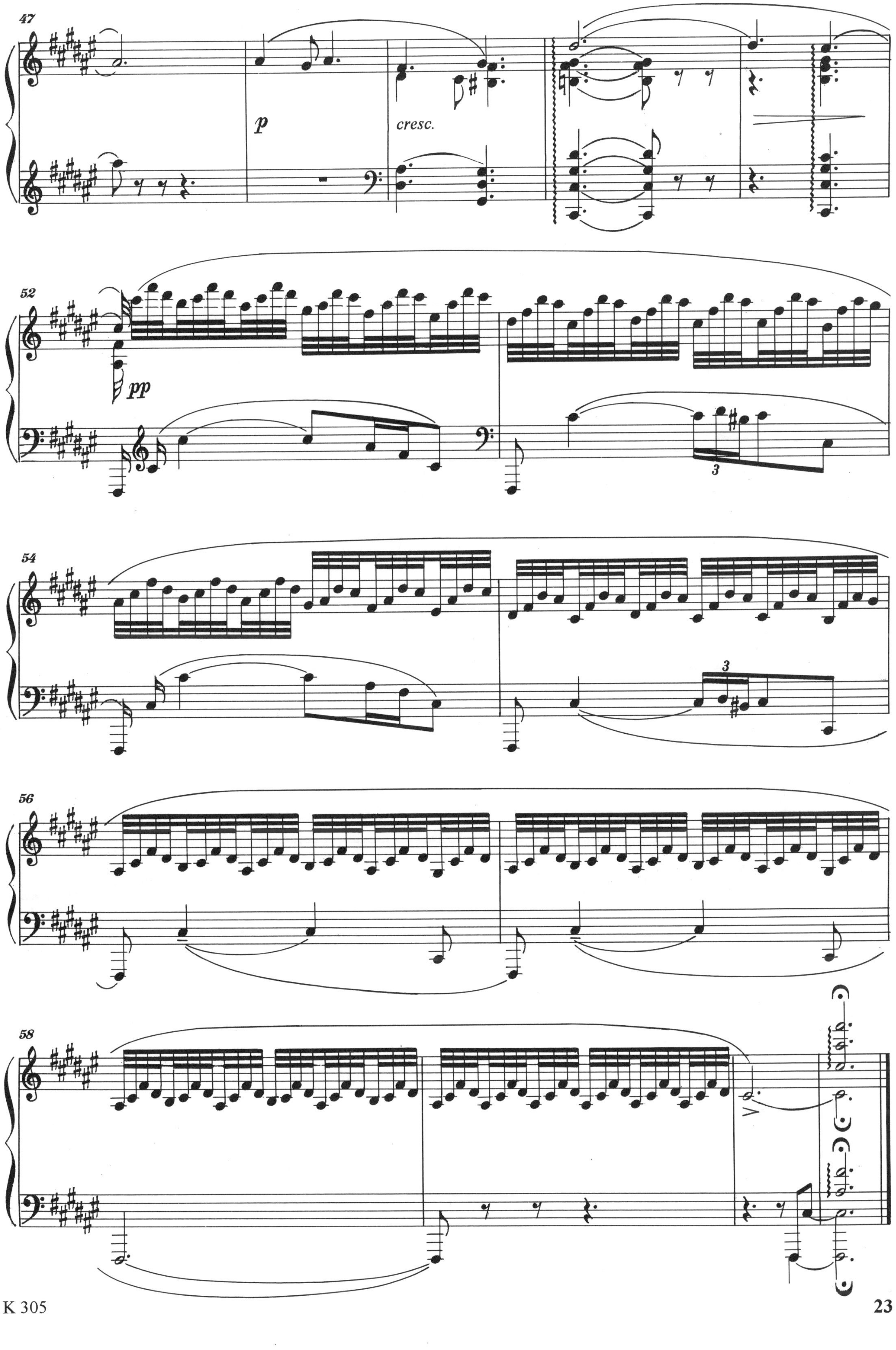
47
p
cresc.
52
pp
54
56
58

Четыре прелюдии   Quatre Préludes

Посвящается Ивану Александровичу Помазанскому

Op.46.
1899

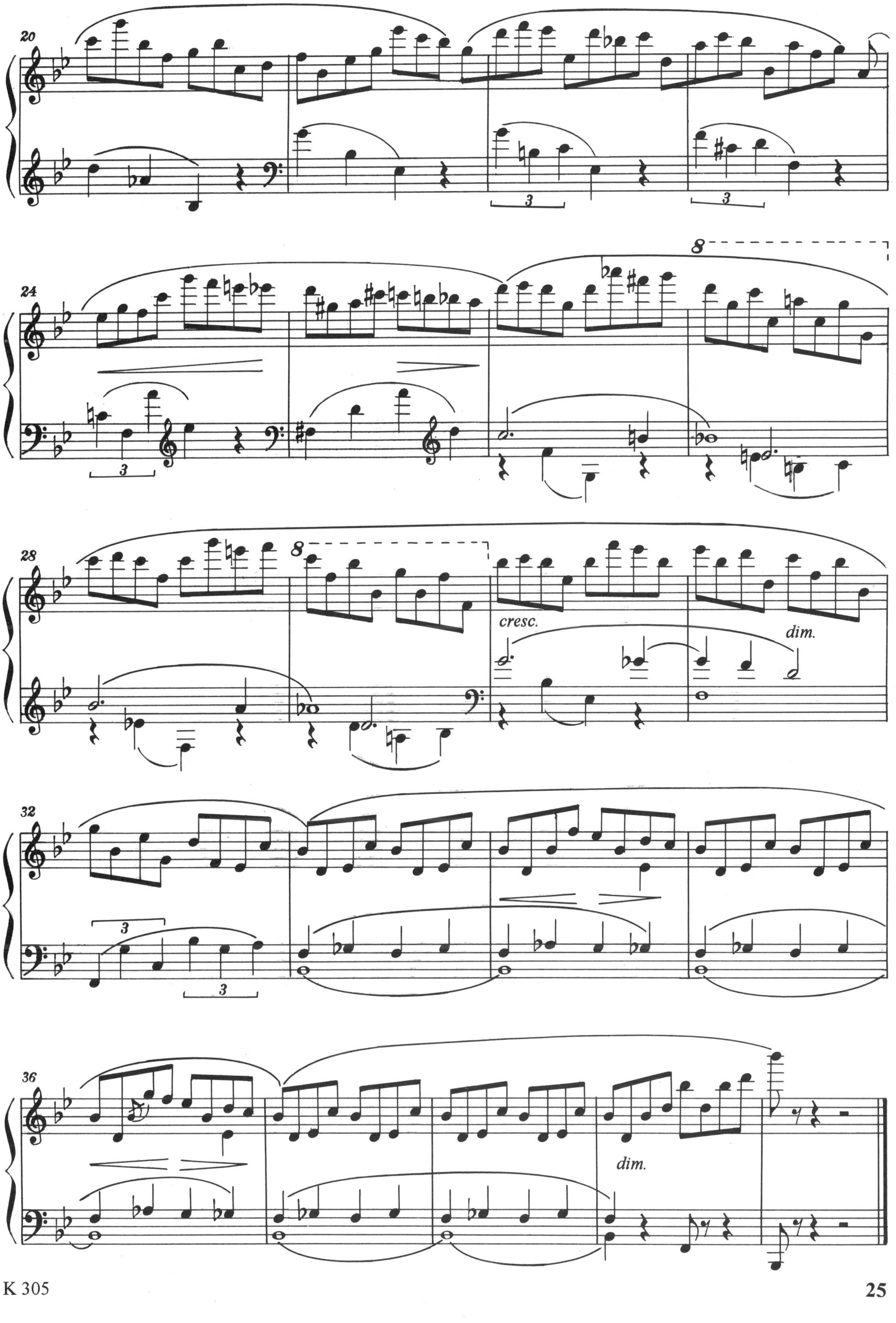
20
24
28
32
36
cresc.
dim.
dim.

Agitato 𝅗𝅥=76
2.
mf
cresc.
f
dim.
rit.
a tempo
mf
cresc.
cresc.
cresc.
f
cresc.
stringendo
a tempo
dim.
p

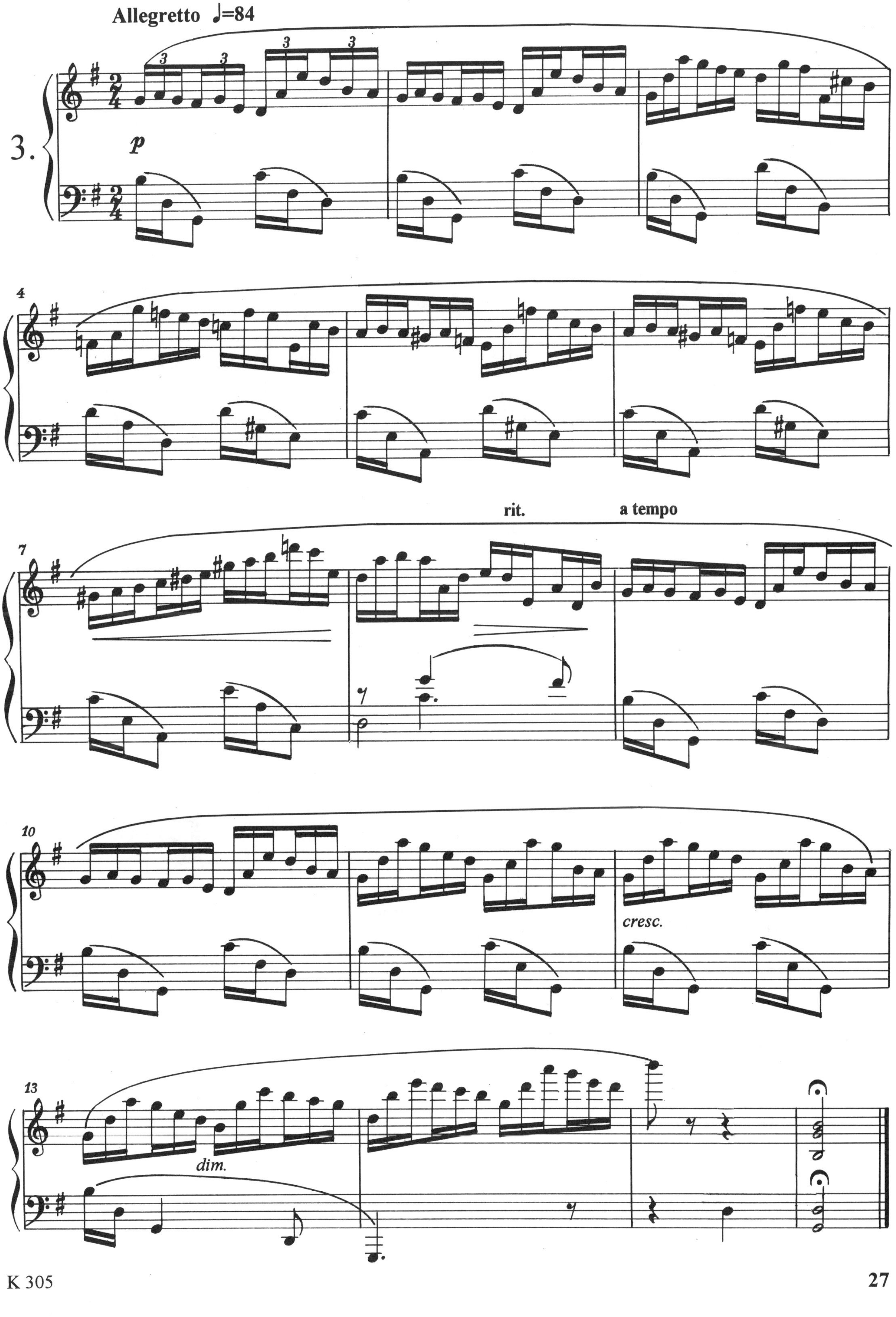
Allegretto ♩=84
3.
p
rit.
a tempo
cresc.
dim.

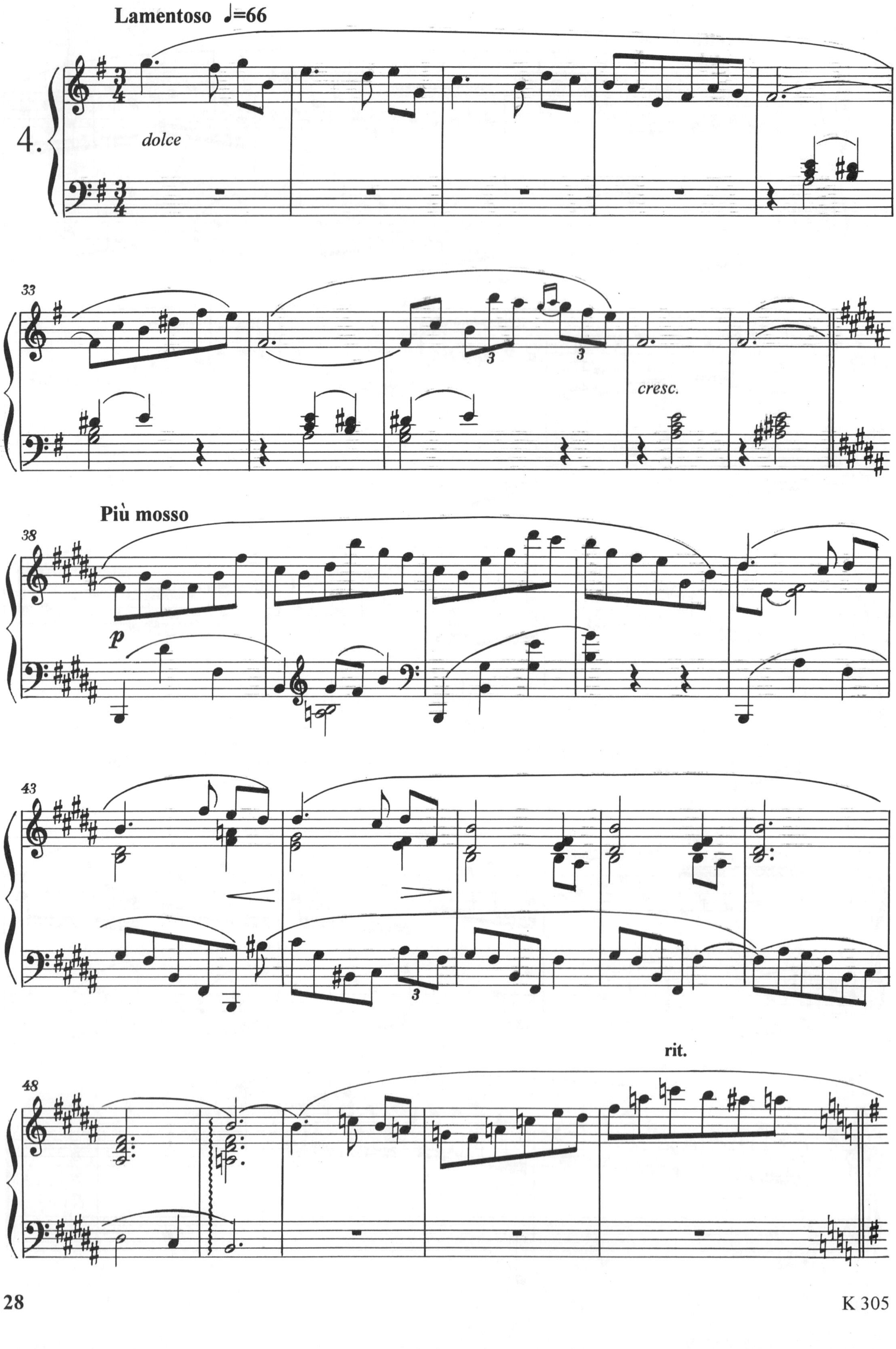
Lamentoso ♩=66
4.
dolce
33
cresc.
Più mosso
38
p
43
48
rit.

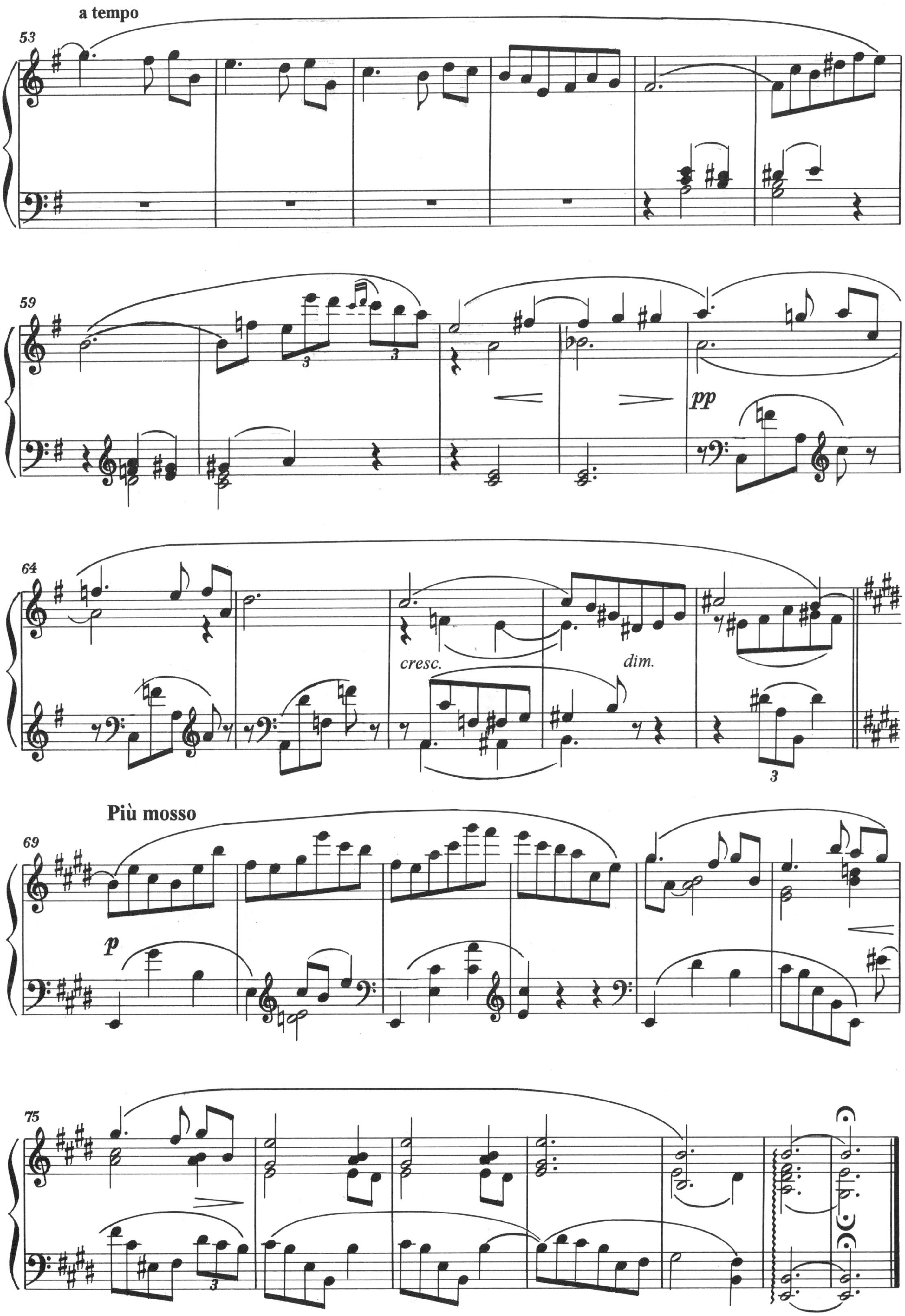
a tempo
53
59
pp
64
cresc.
dim.
Più mosso
69
p
75

Этюд и канцонетта — Étude et Canzonetta

Dédié à Monsieur Alexandre Ziloti

Op. 48.
1899

Этюд — Étude

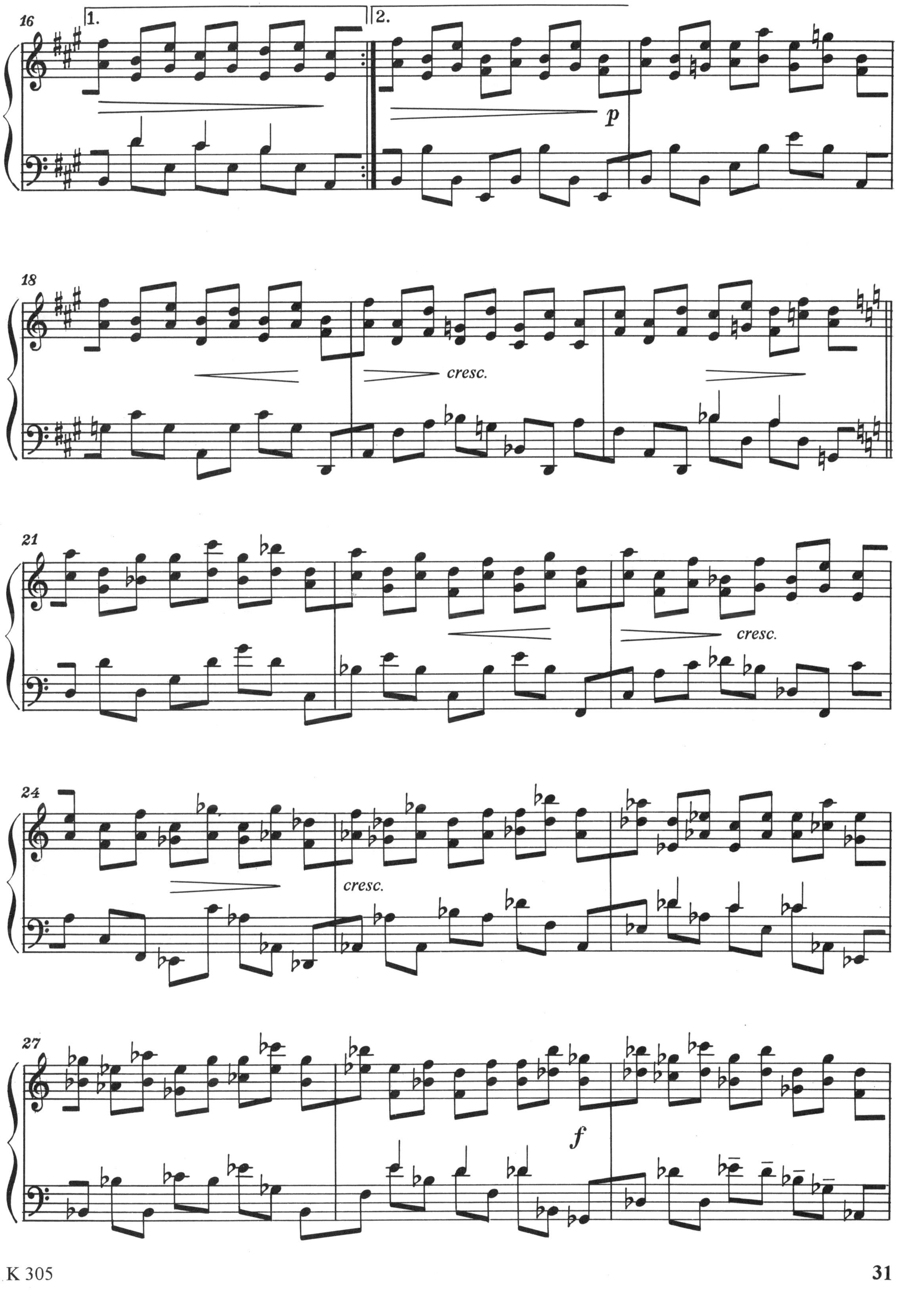
16
1.
2.
p
18
cresc.
21
cresc.
24
cresc.
27
f

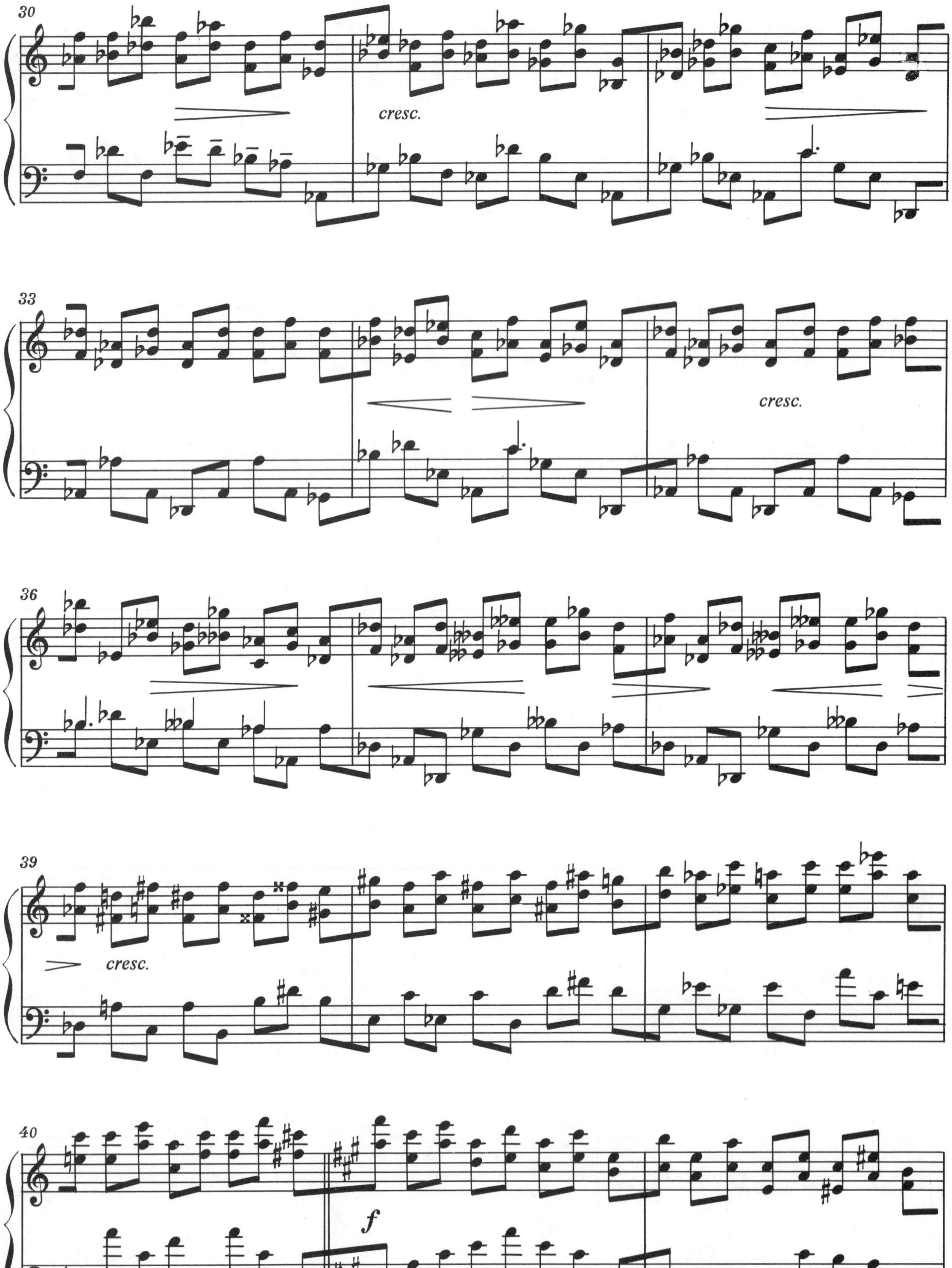
30
cresc.
33
cresc.
36
39
cresc.
40
f

K 305

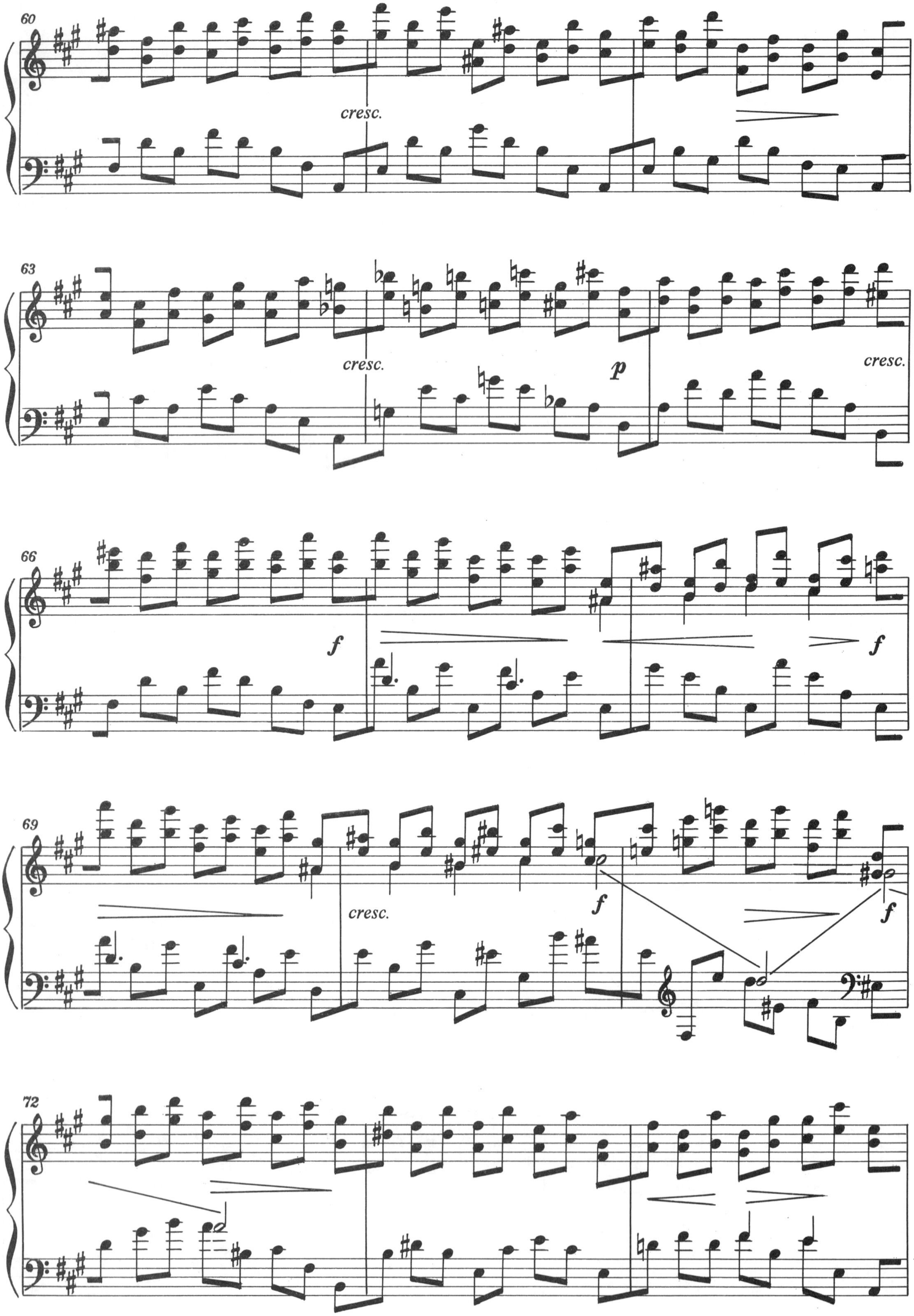
60
cresc.
63
cresc.
p
cresc.
66
f
f
69
cresc.
f
f
72

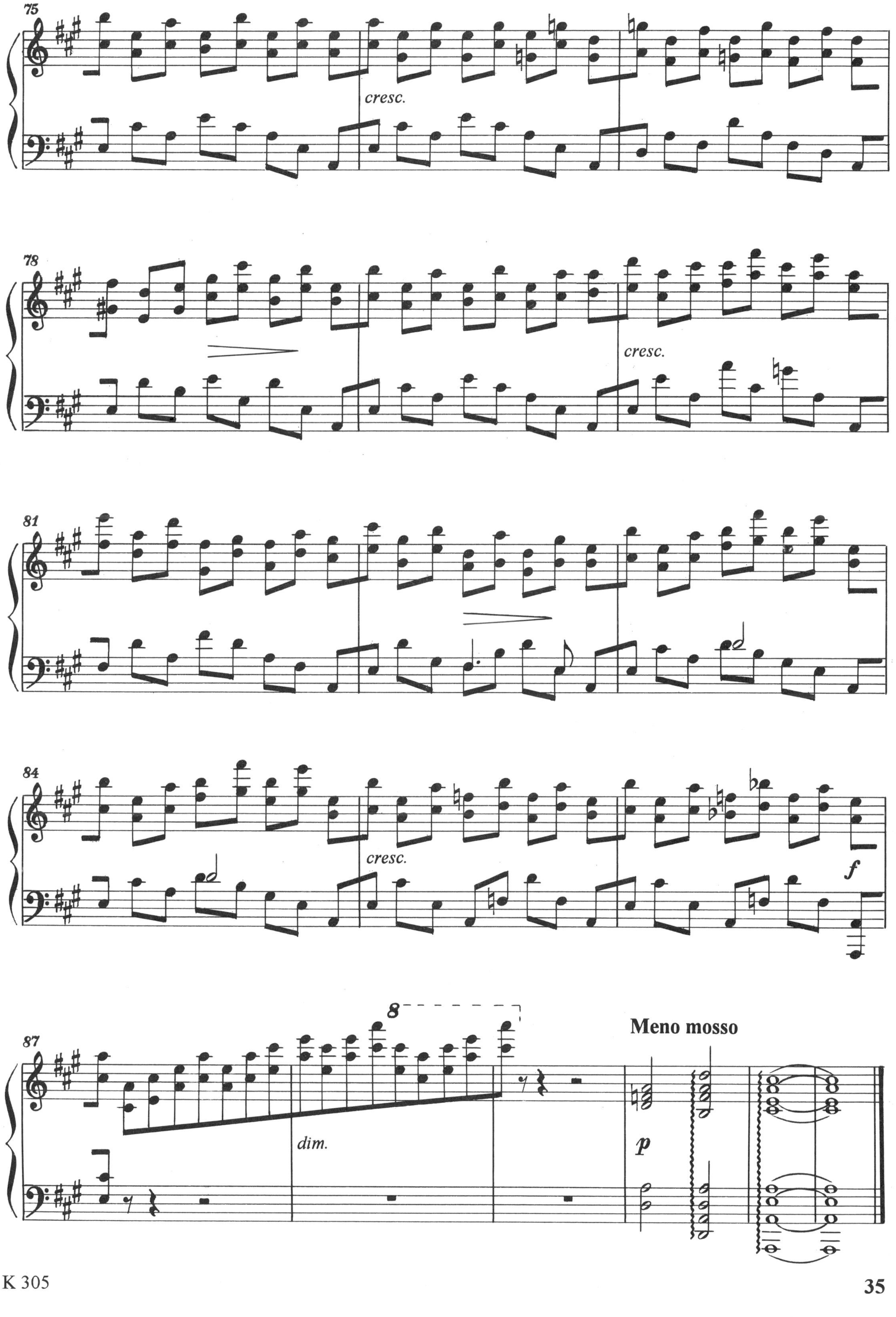
75
cresc.
78
cresc.
81
84
cresc.
f
87
8
dim.
Meno mosso
p

Канцонетта   Canzonetta

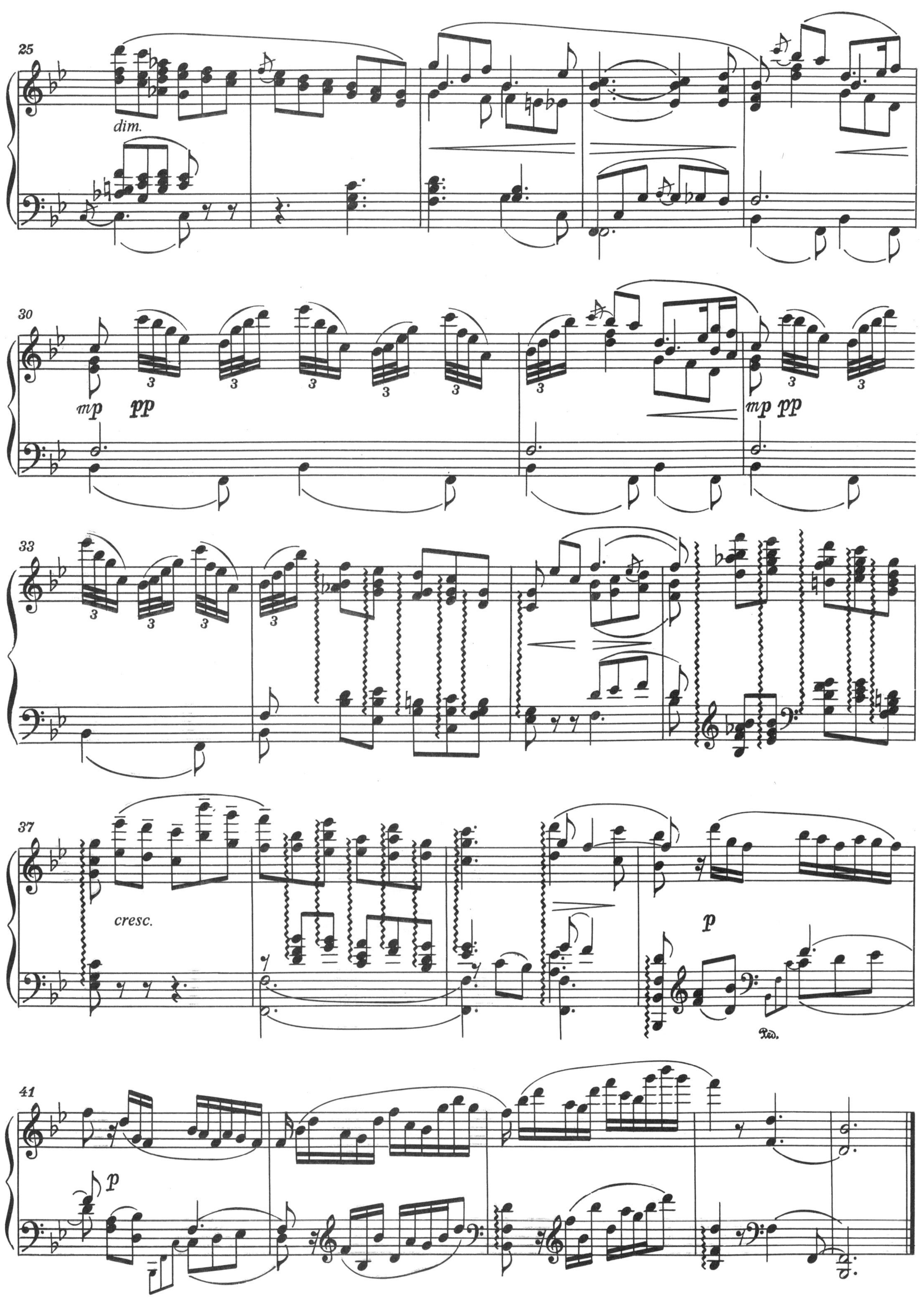
25
dim.
30
mp
pp
mp pp
33
37
cresc.
p
41
p

Вариации на польскую народную песню
Variations sur un thème populaire polonais

A Madame Sophie Poznanska-Rabcewitsch

Op.51.
1901

Var.II

Scherzando ♩=144

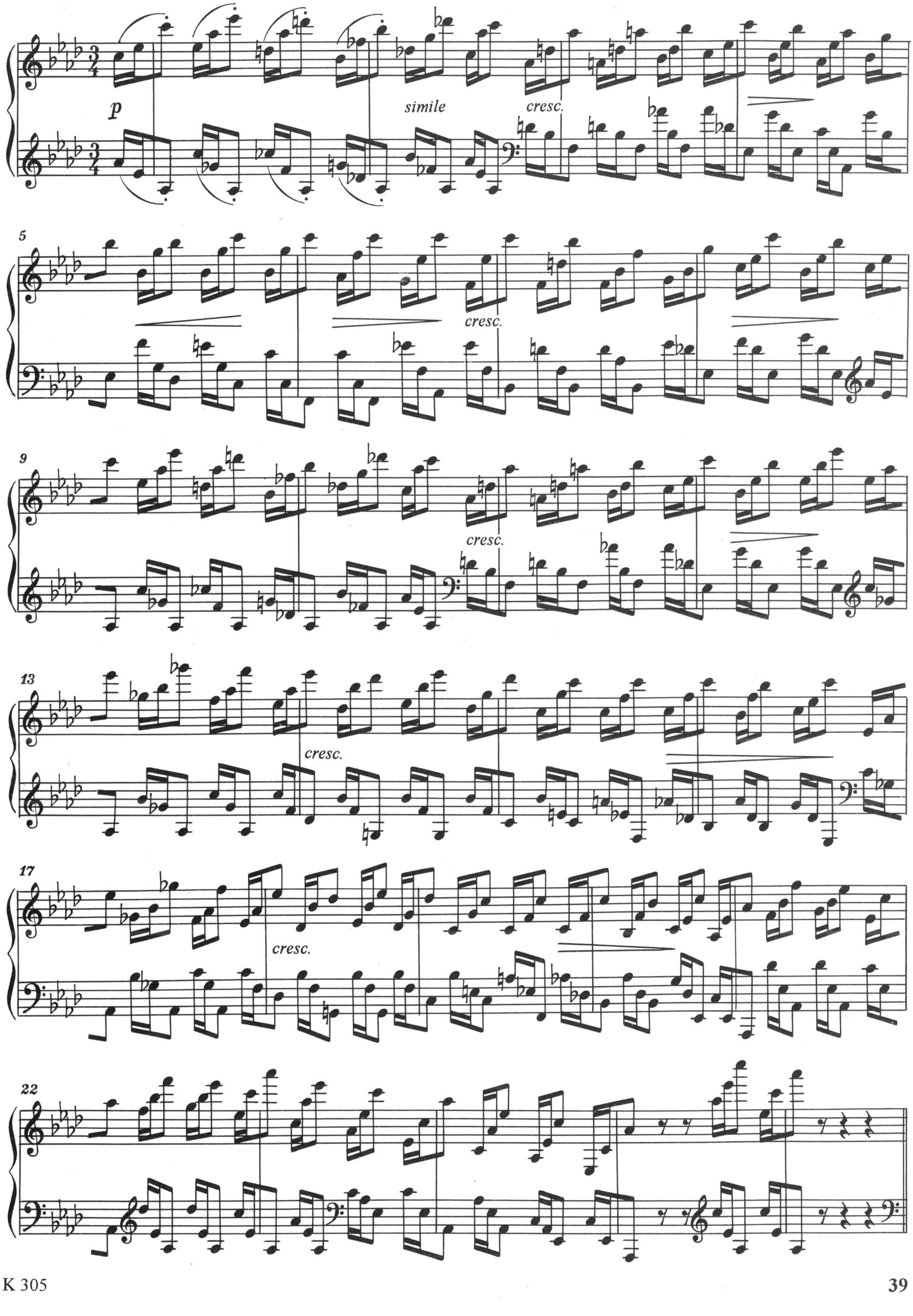

Var.III

Andante ♩=66
p
dolce
cresc.
cresc.
cresc.
cresc.
rit.
a tempo
p
cresc.
cresc.

Var. IV **Allegretto** ♩=106

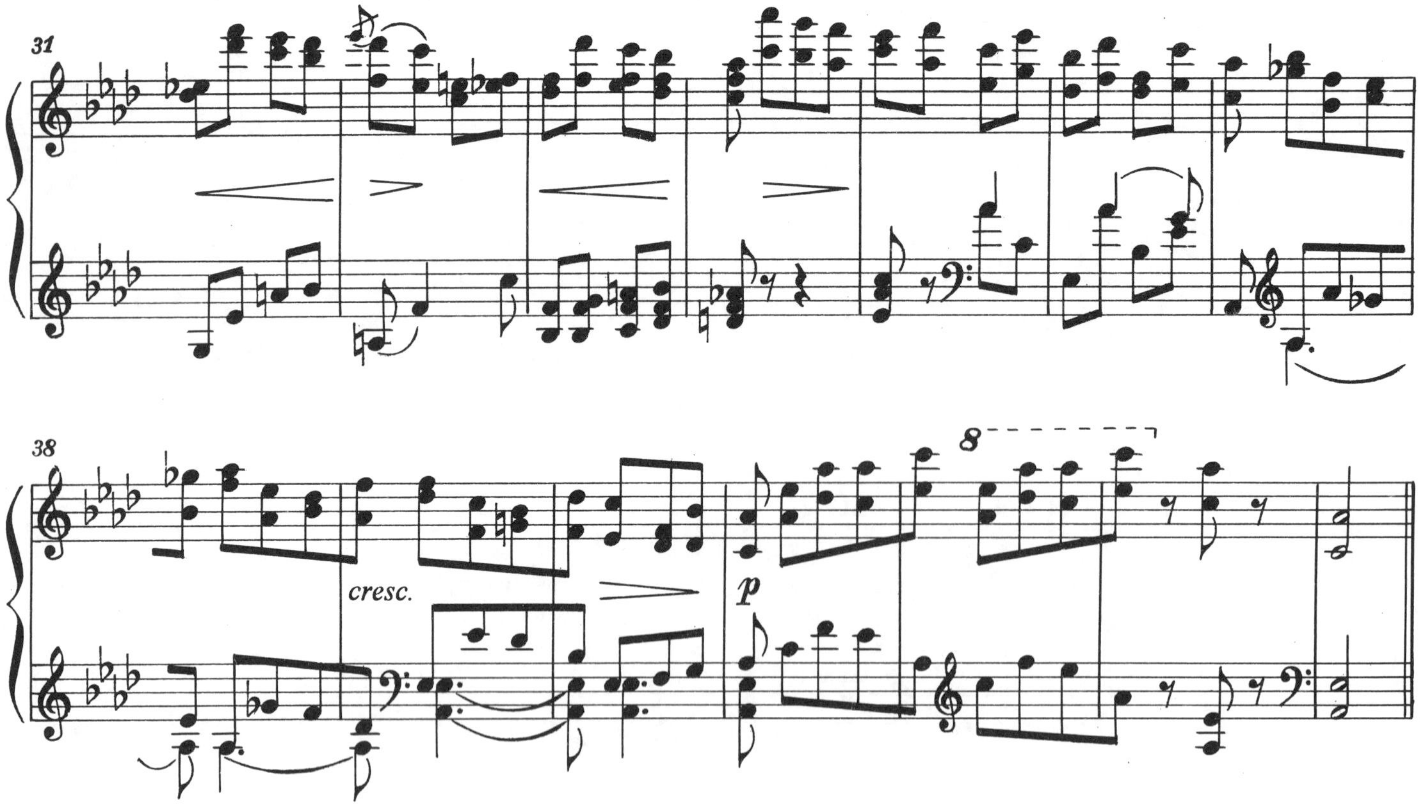

Var. V

Veloce ♩=104

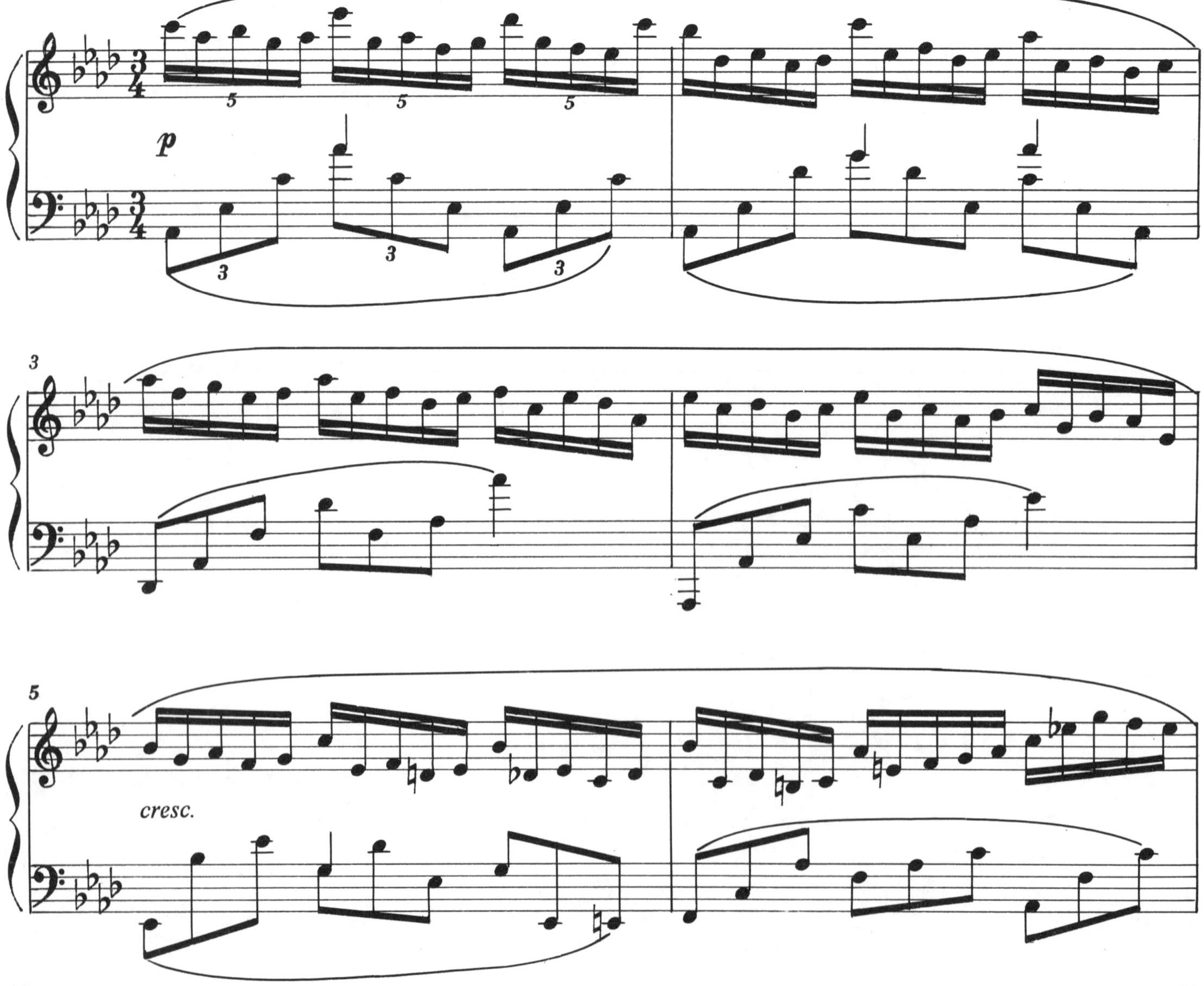

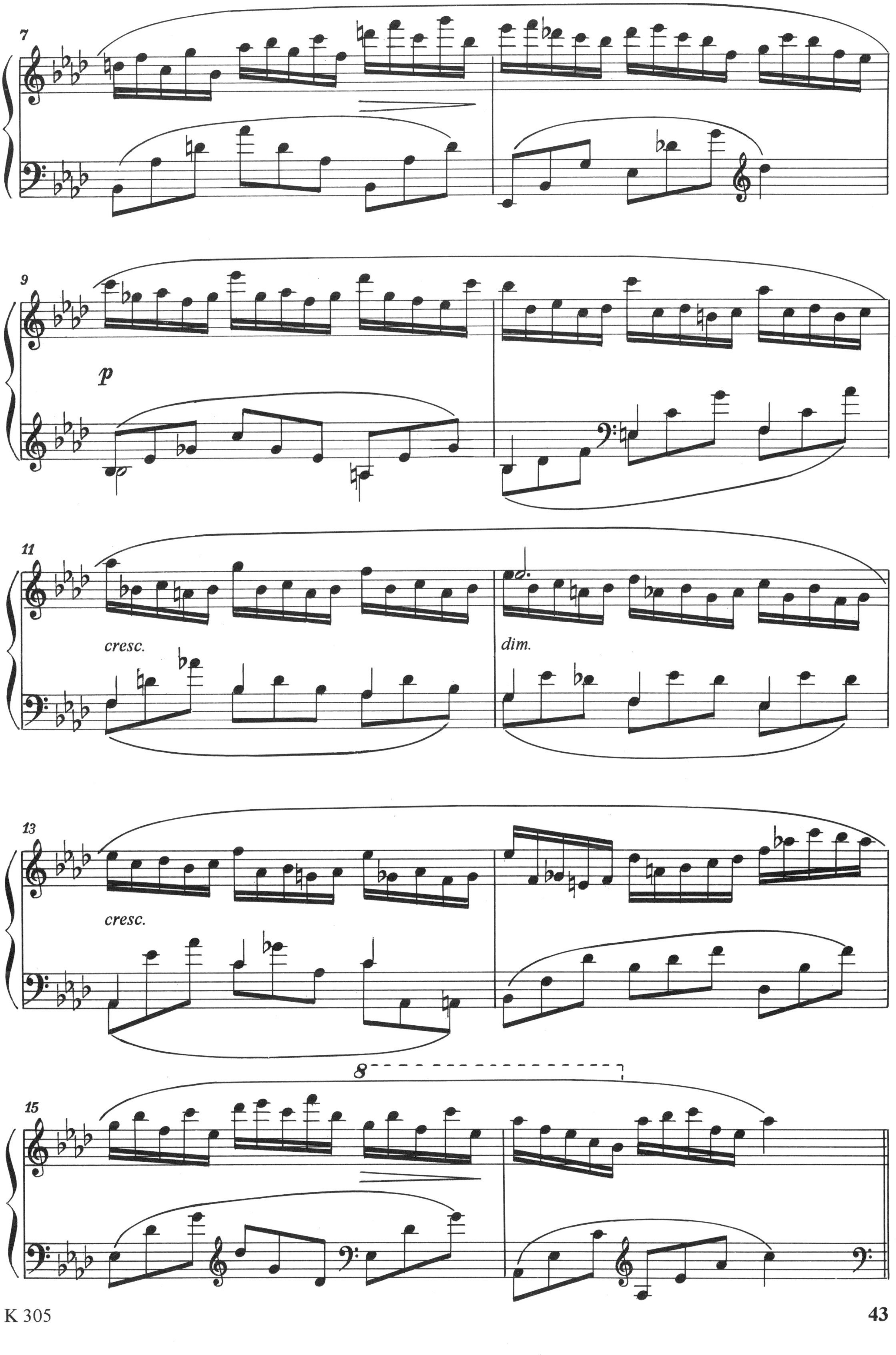
7
9
p
11
cresc.
dim.
13
cresc.
8
15

Var. VI **Andante pastorale** ♩=56

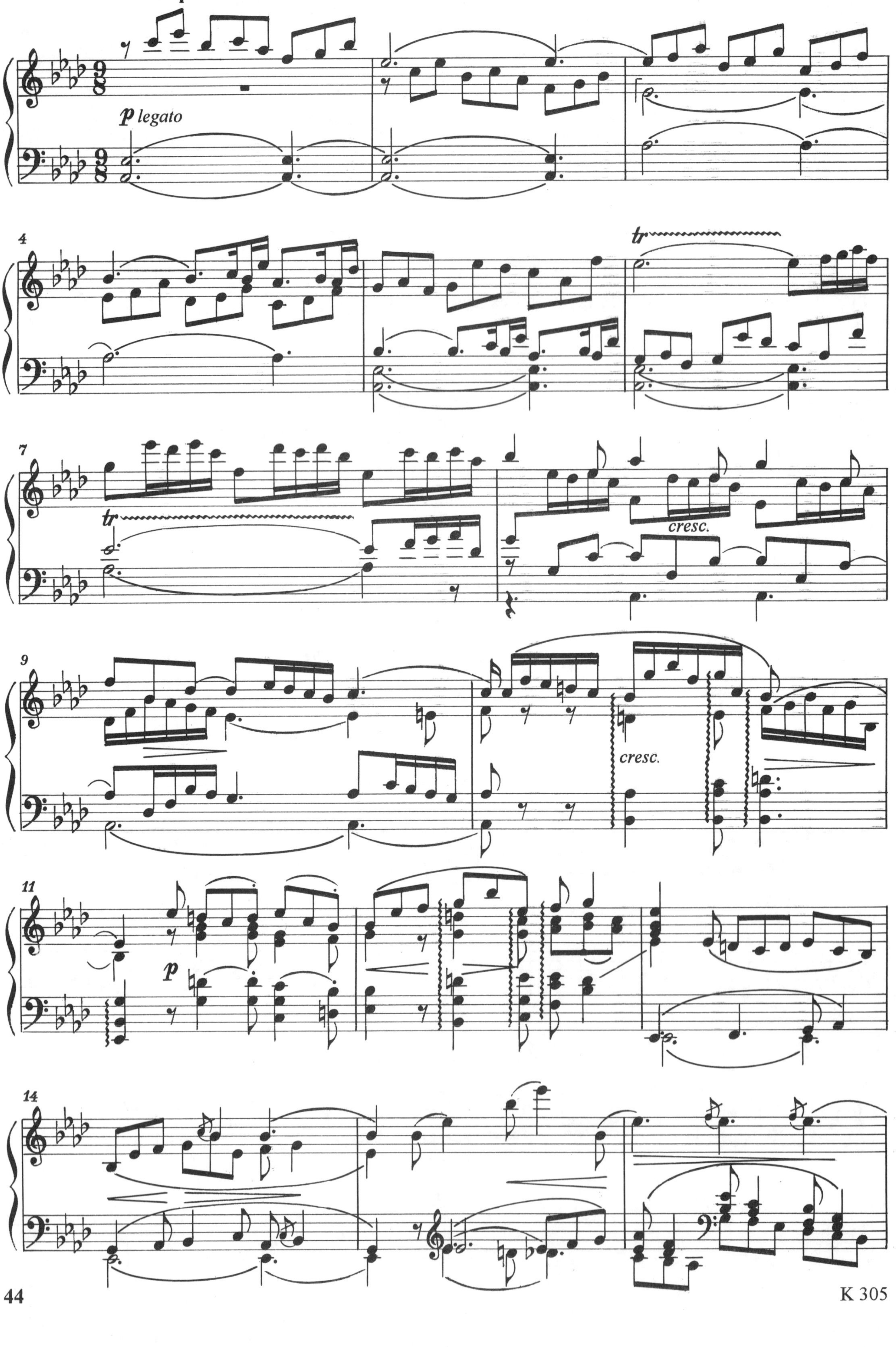

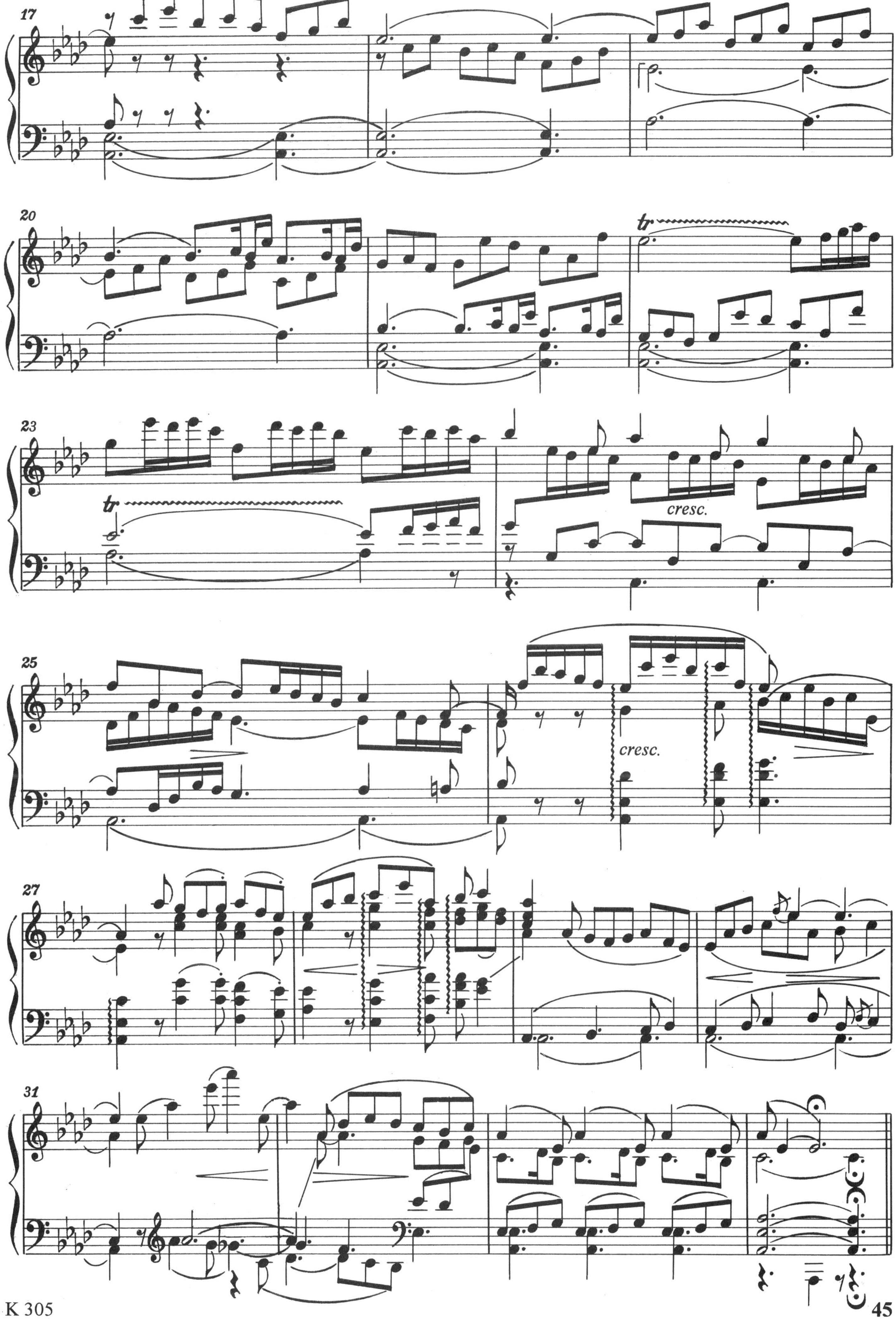
17
20
tr
23
tr
cresc.
25
cresc.
27
31

Var. VII

Allegro con fuoco ♩=132

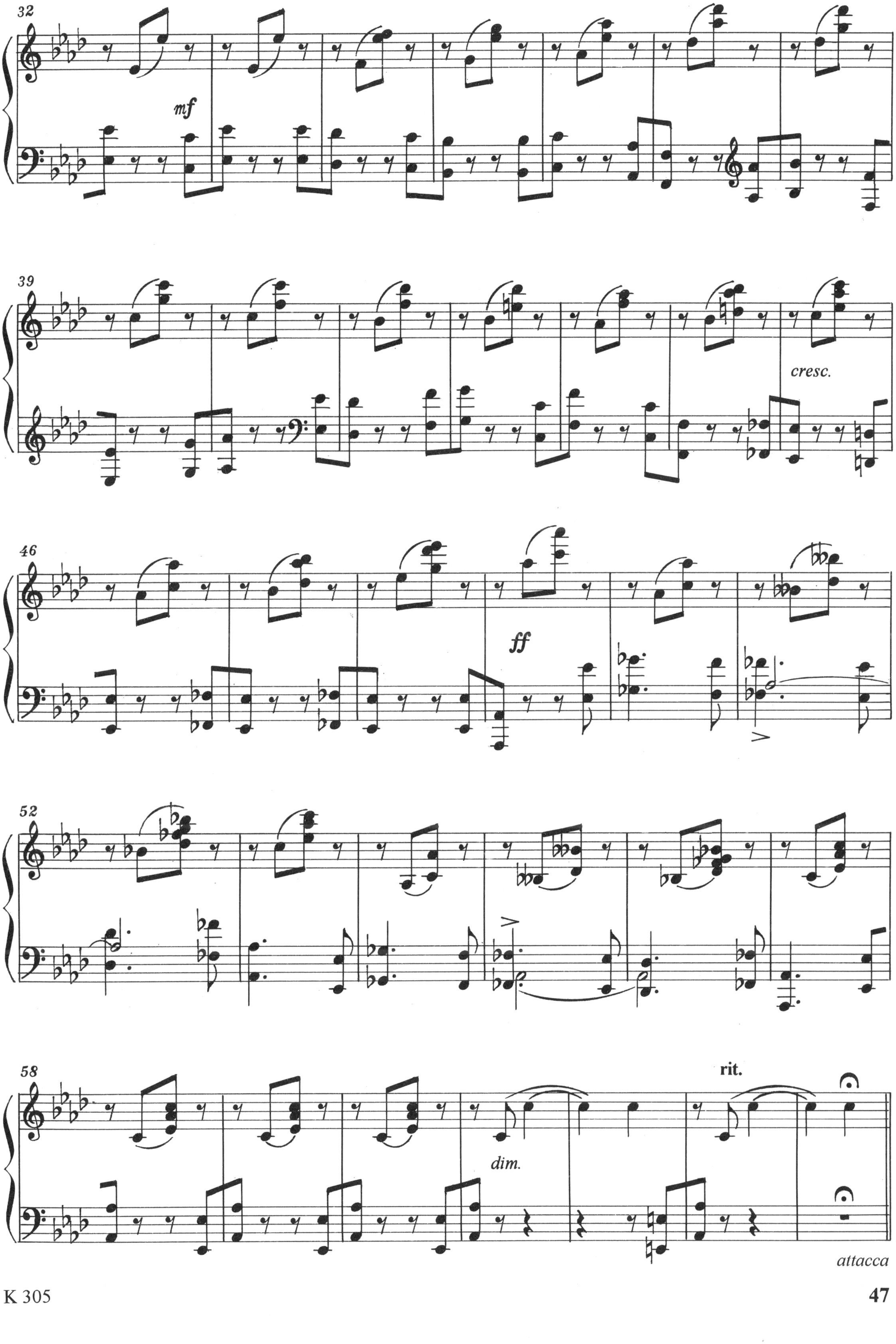
32
mf
39
cresc.
46
ff
52
58
rit.
dim.
attacca

Var. VIII

Andantino ♩=108

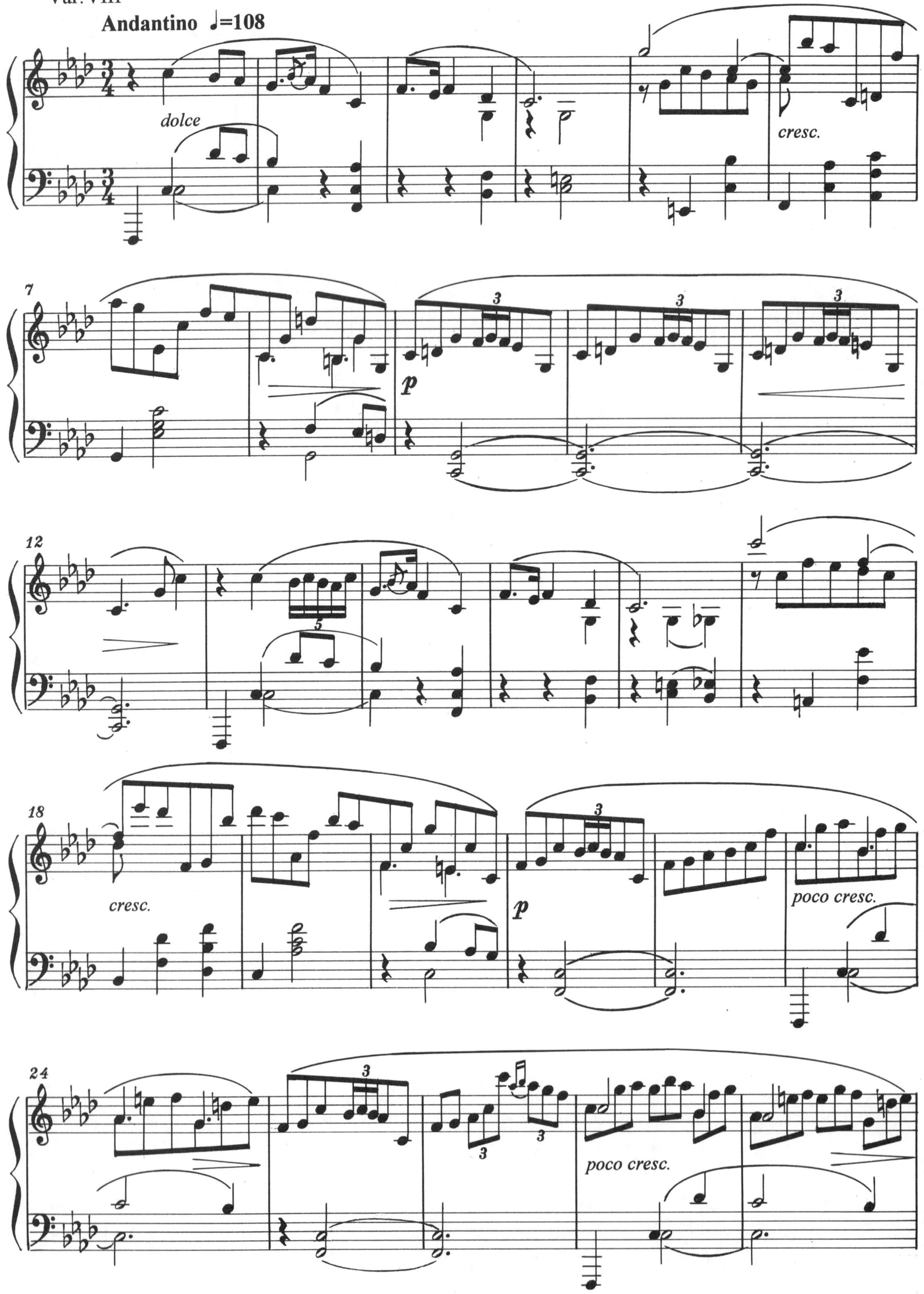

Var. IX
Soave ♪=132

Var.X
Moderato ♩=84
poco a poco accelerando
f
p
cresc.
6
8
f
dim.
11
Allegretto ♩=100
mf
3
17
p
cresc.
22
rit.
a tempo
cresc.
f
rit.
a tempo
27
p
3
3

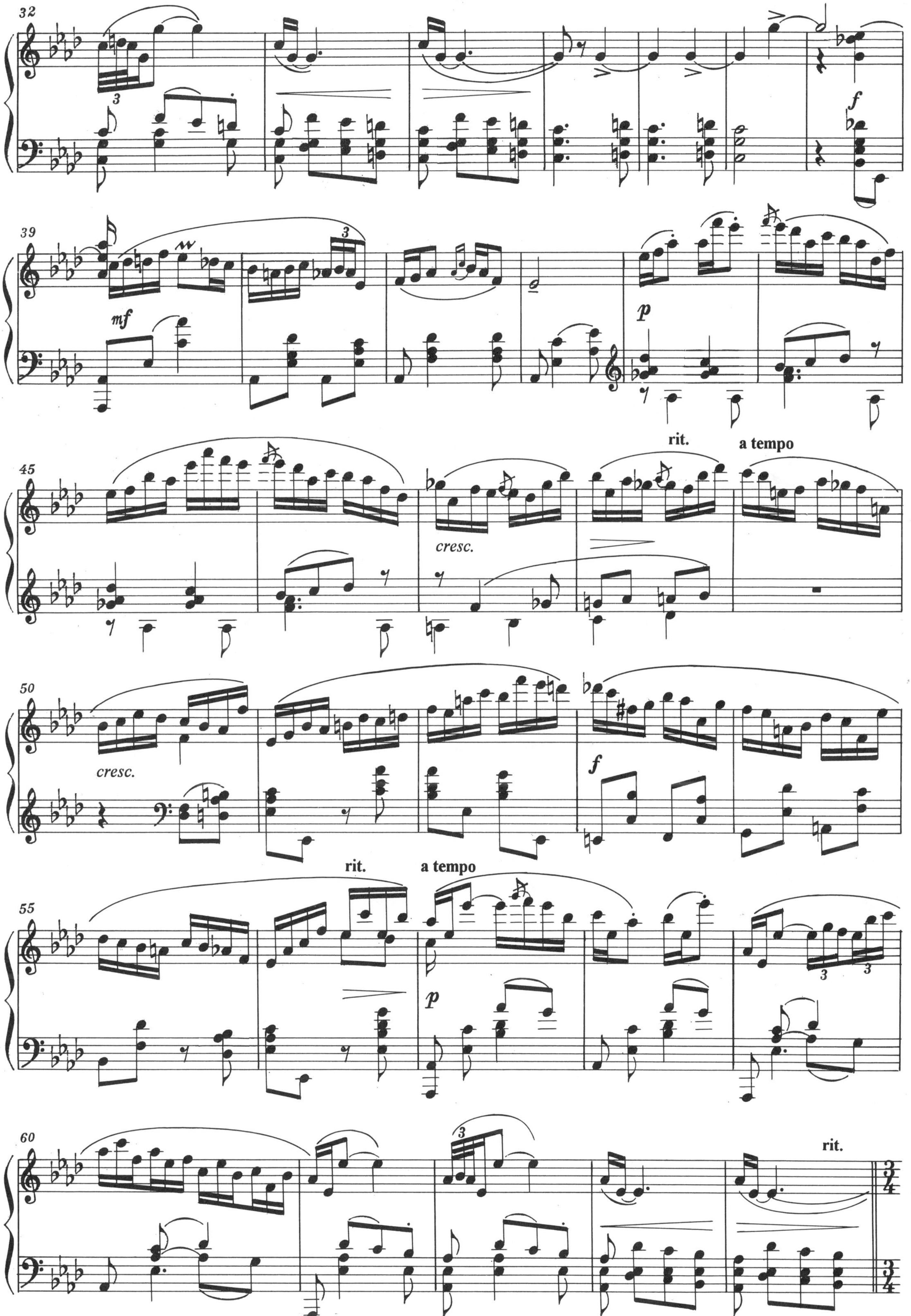

rit.
a tempo
cresc.
cresc.
rit.
a tempo
rit.

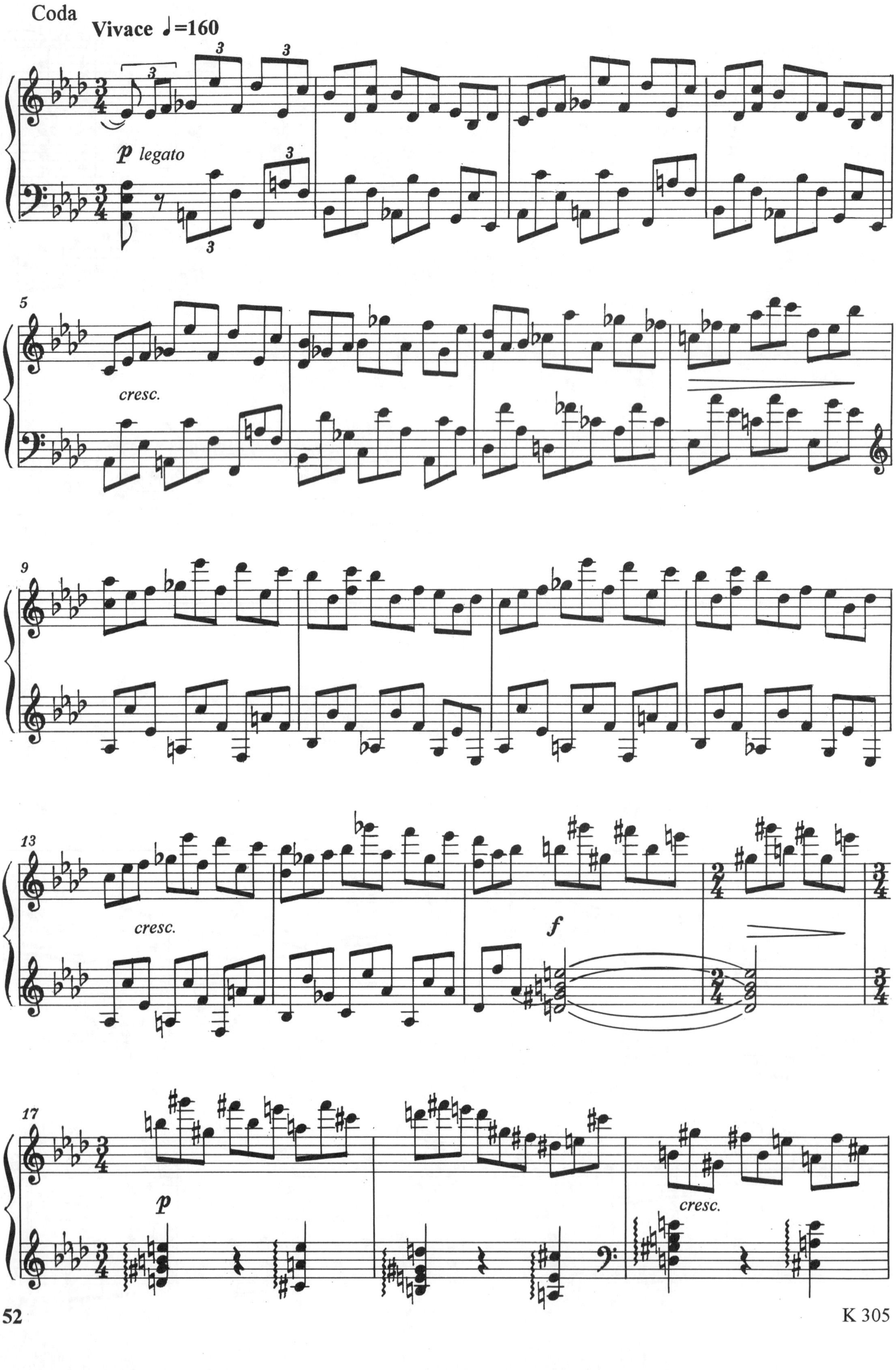
Coda
Vivace ♩=160
p legato
cresc.
cresc.
f
p
cresc.

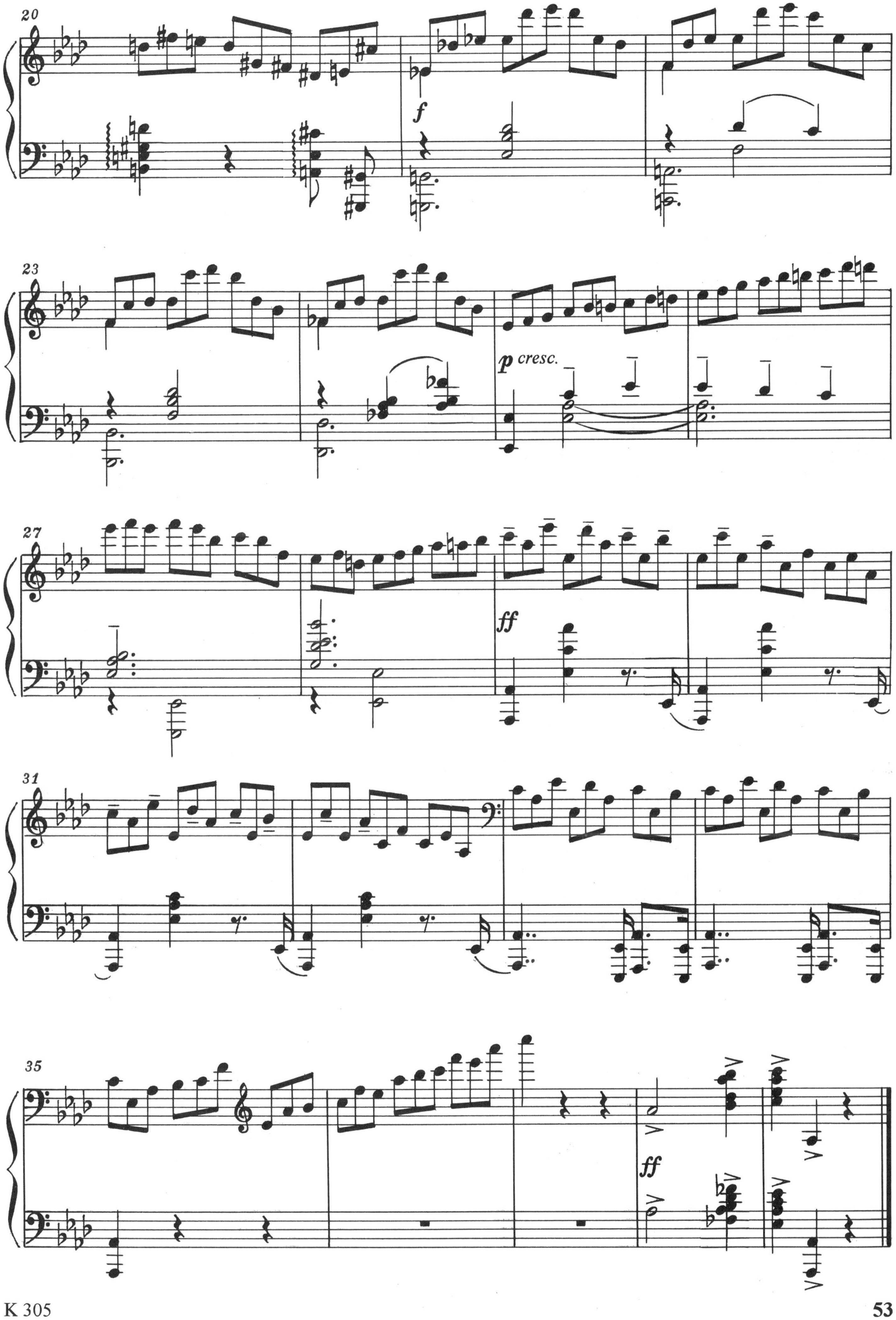
20
f
23
p cresc.
27
ff
31
35
ff

Три балетных номера
Trois Morceaux de ballet

Посвящается Владимиру Александровичу Авдееву

Op.52.
1901

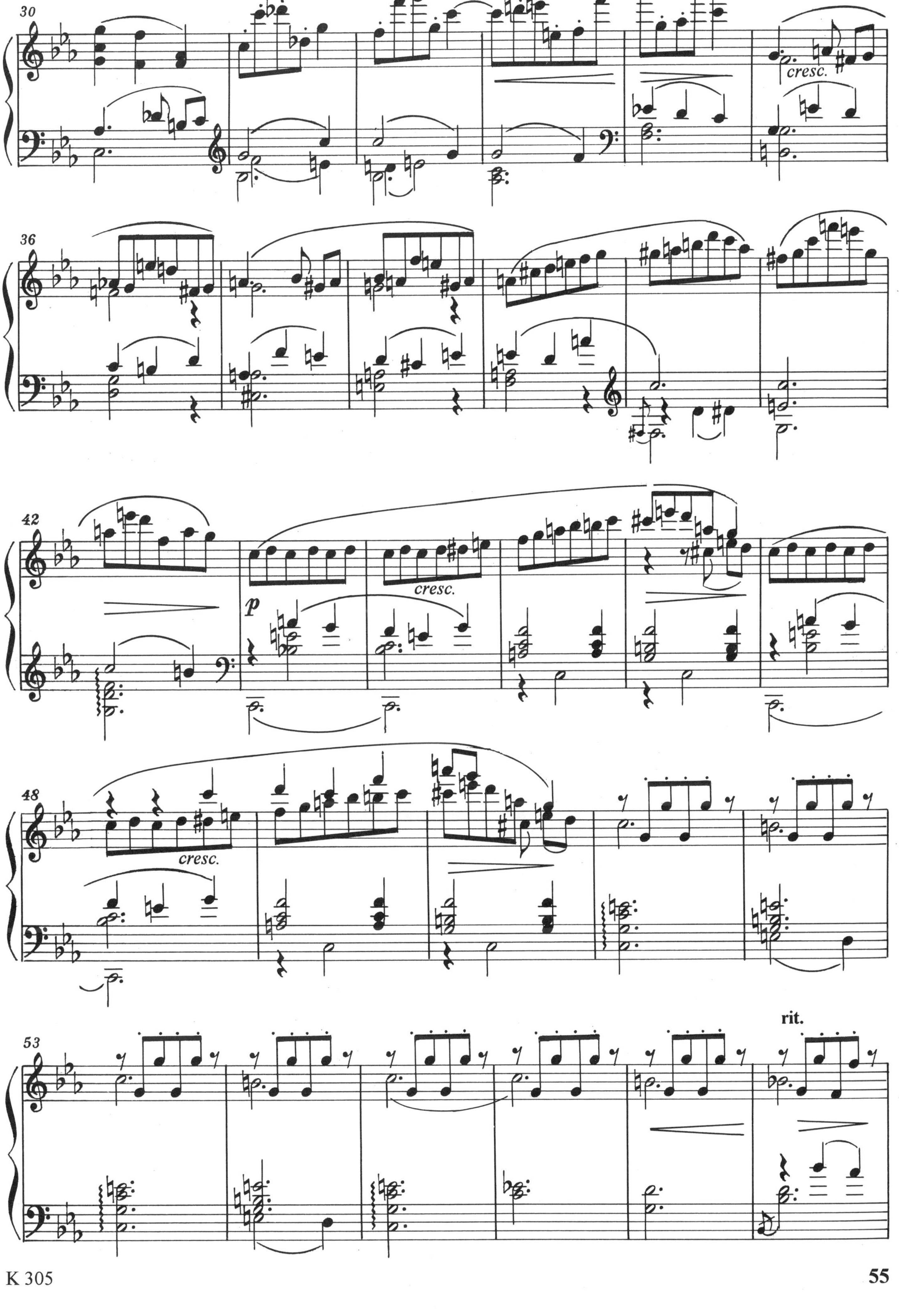
30
cresc.
36
42
cresc.
p
48
cresc.
53
rit.

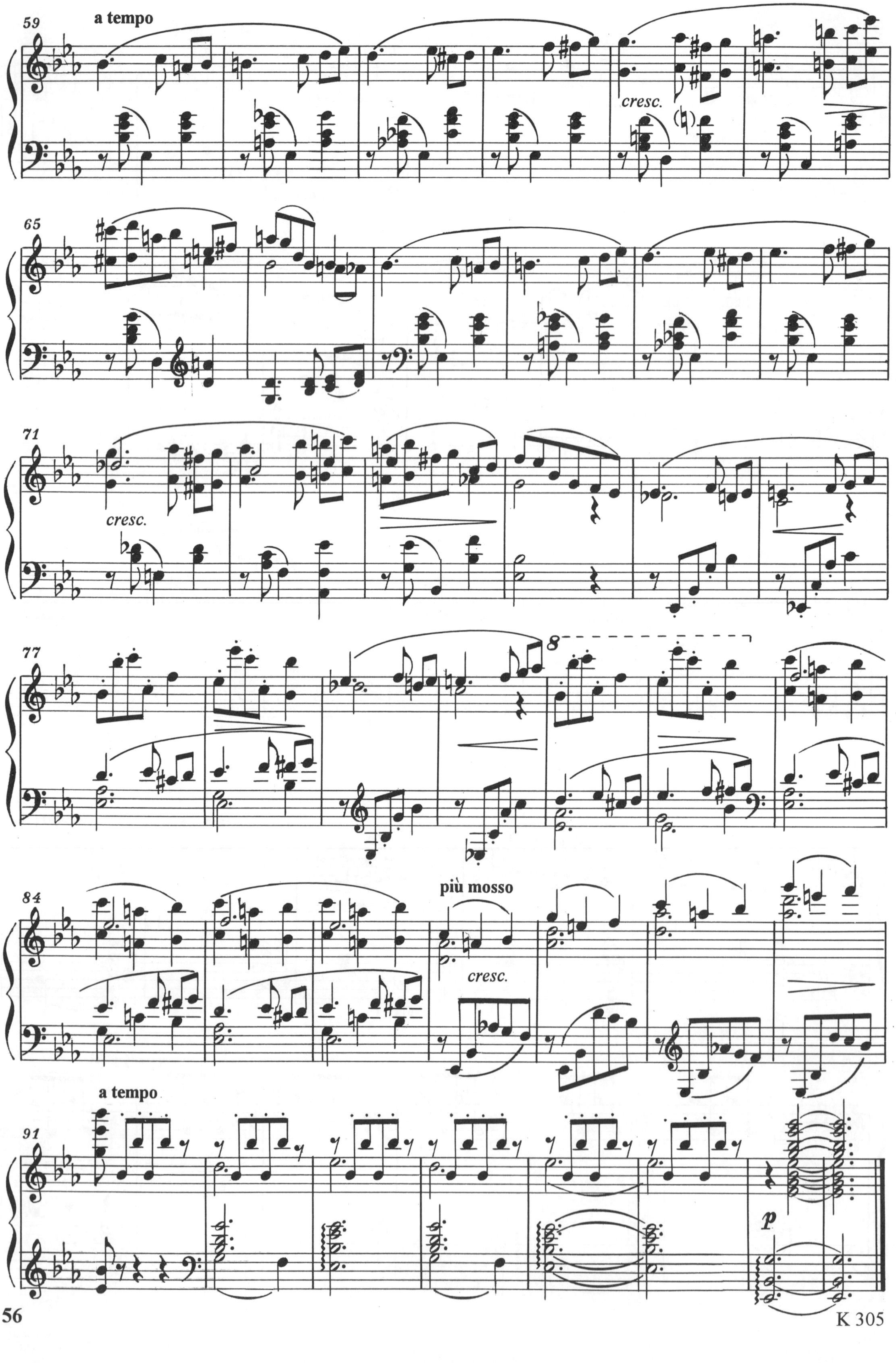
a tempo
cresc.
più mosso
cresc.
a tempo
p

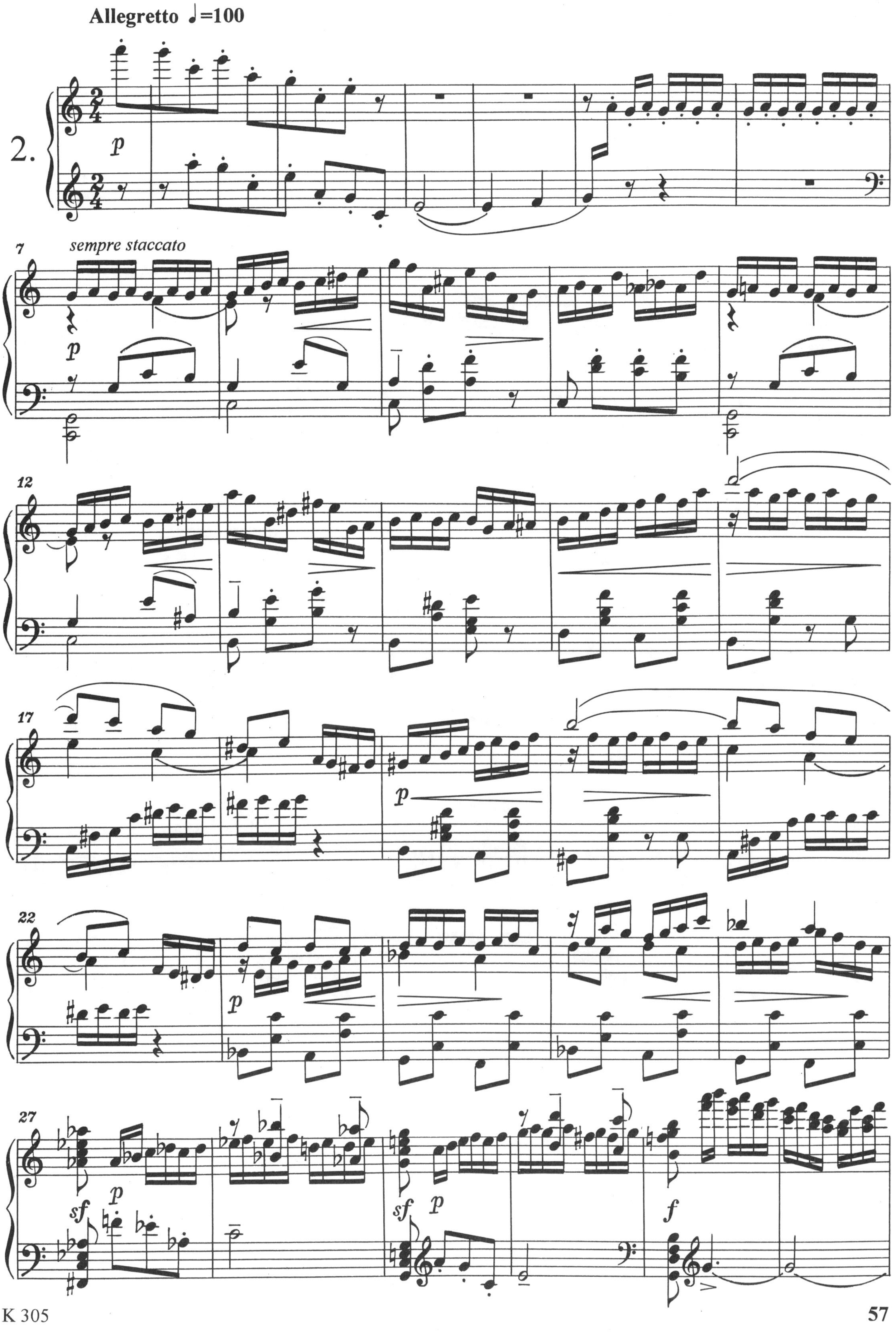
Allegretto ♩=100
2.
p
sempre staccato
sf
f

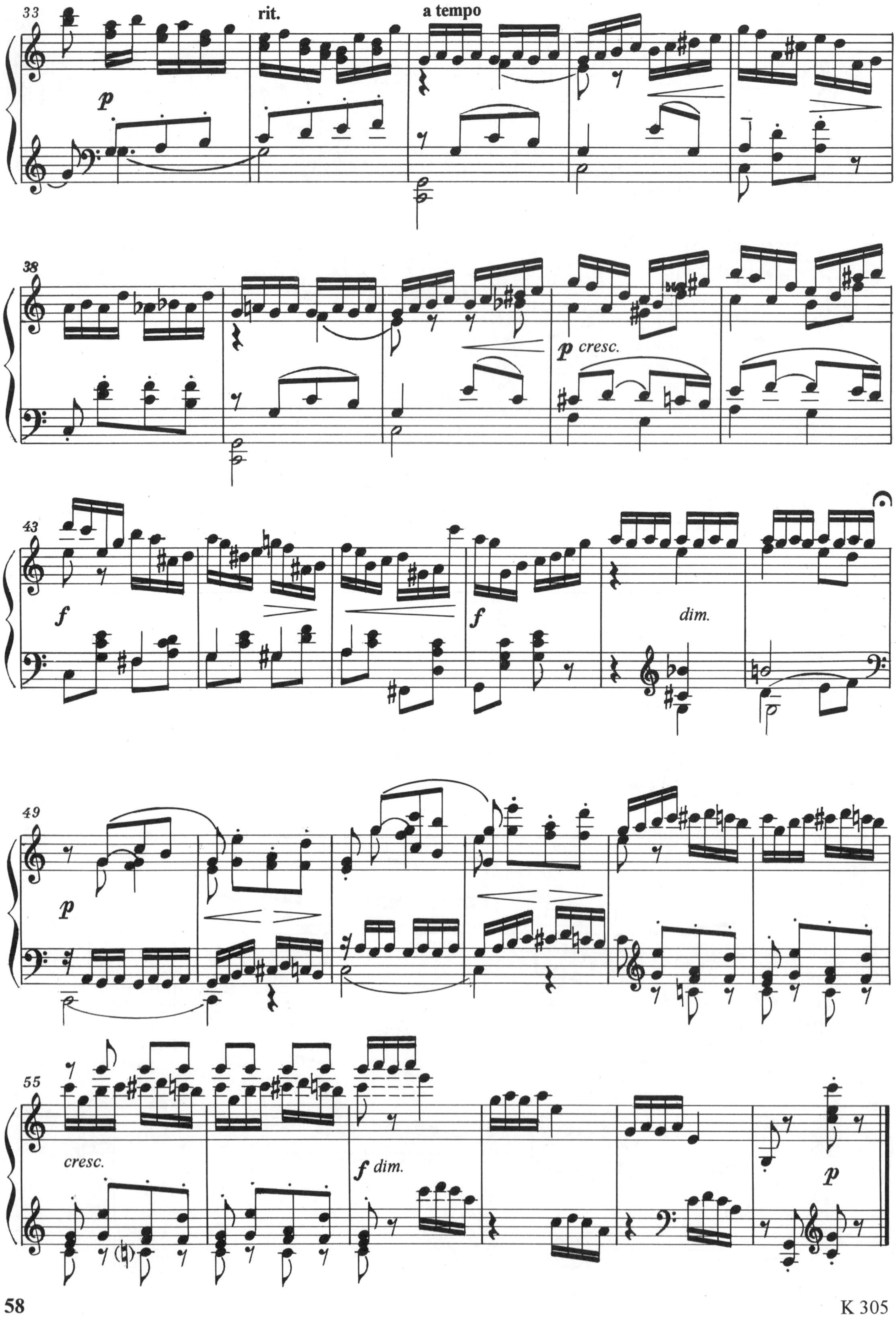
rit.
a tempo
cresc.
dim.
cresc.
dim.

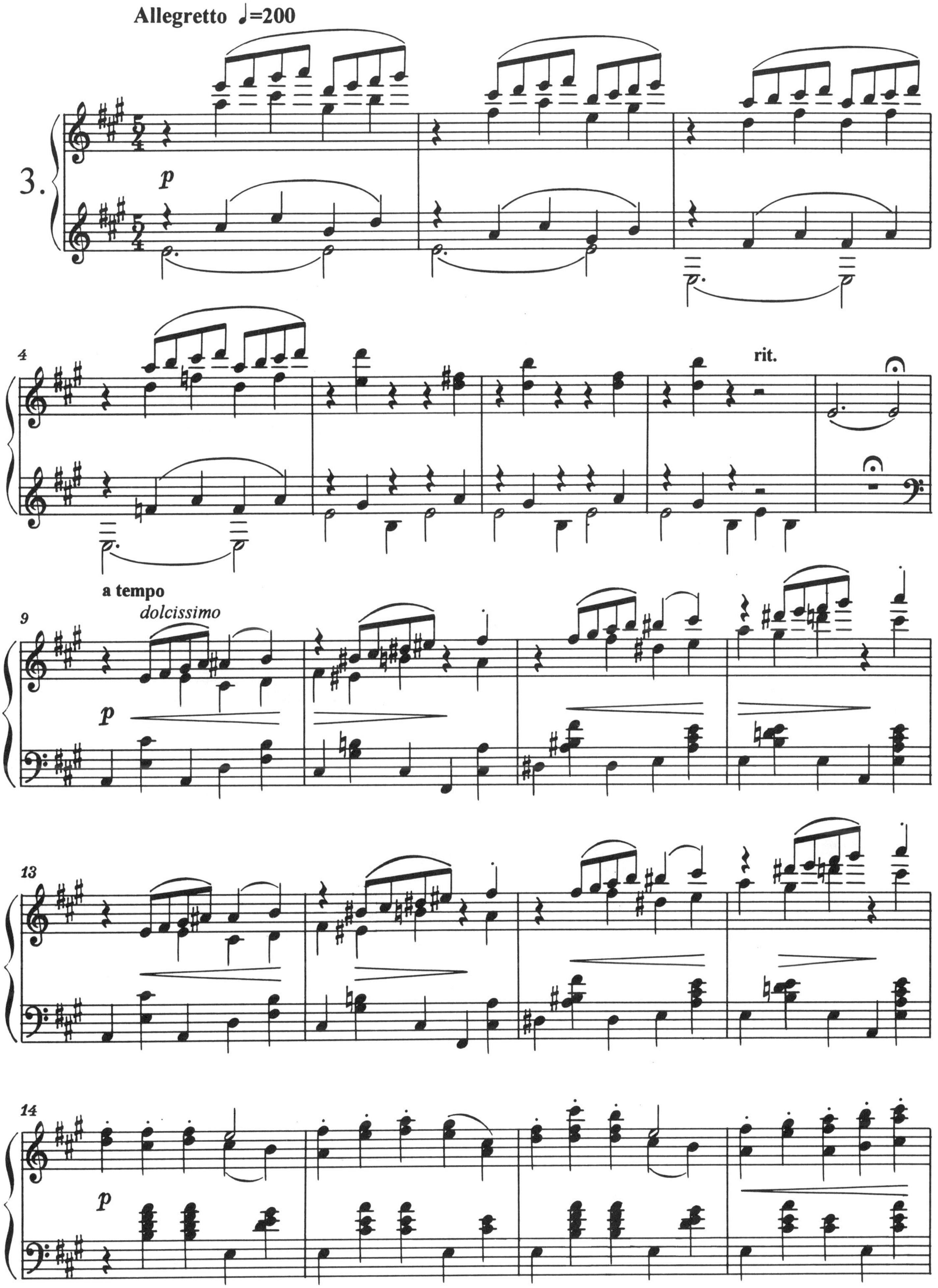
Allegretto ♩=200
3.
p
4
rit.
a tempo
dolcissimo
9
p
13
14
p

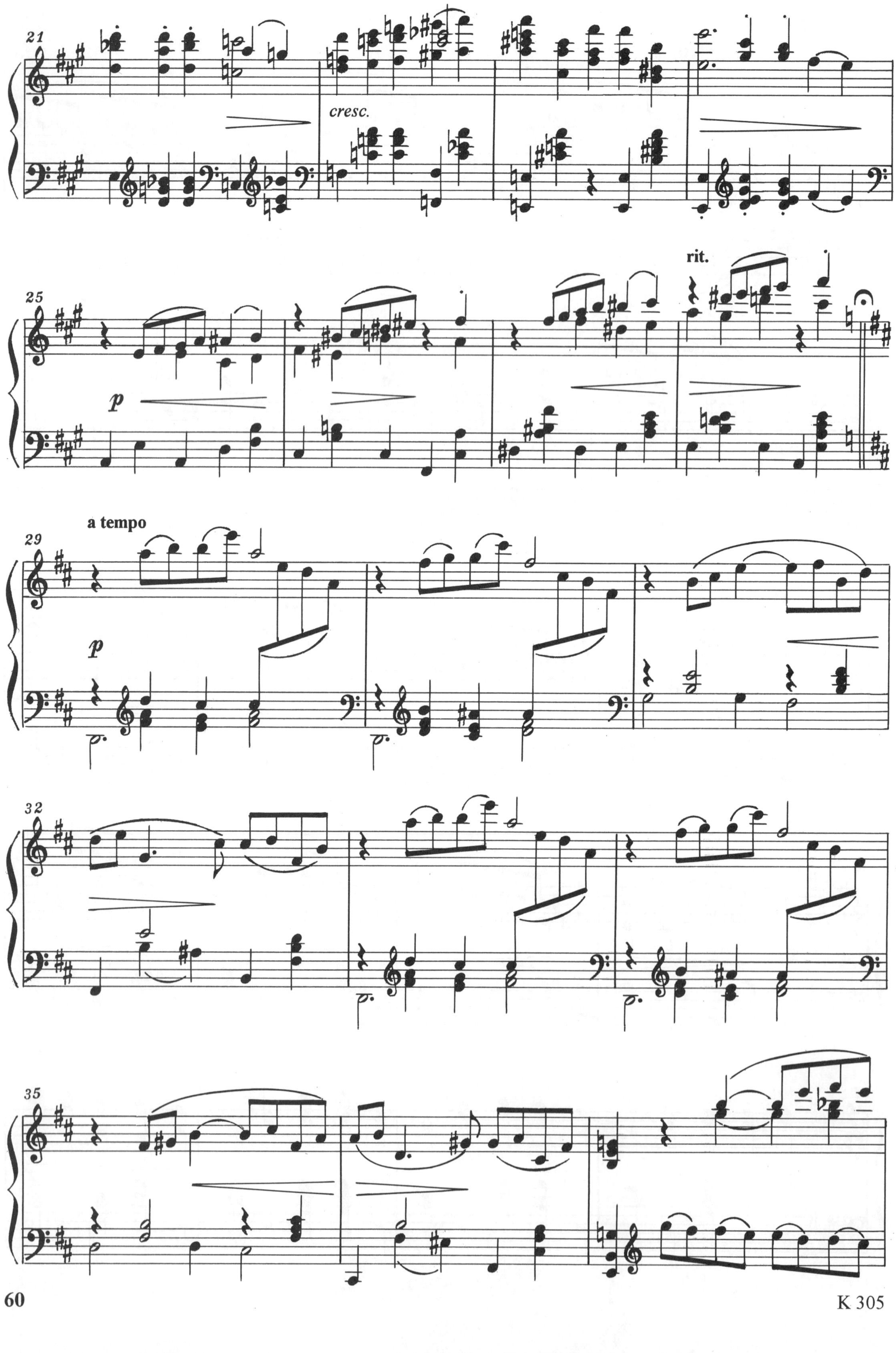
21
cresc.
25
p
rit.
29
a tempo
p
32
35

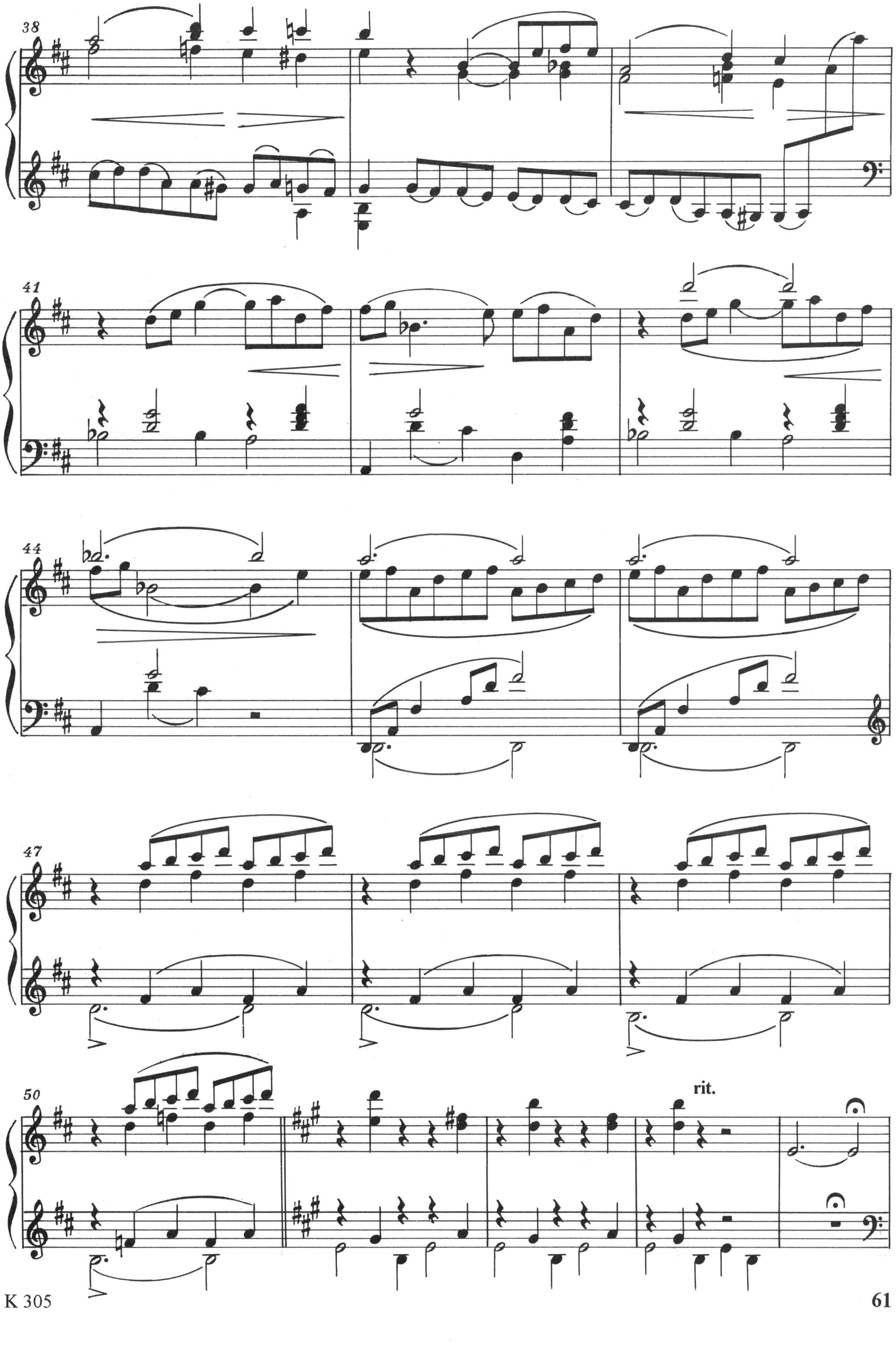
38
41
44
47
50
rit.

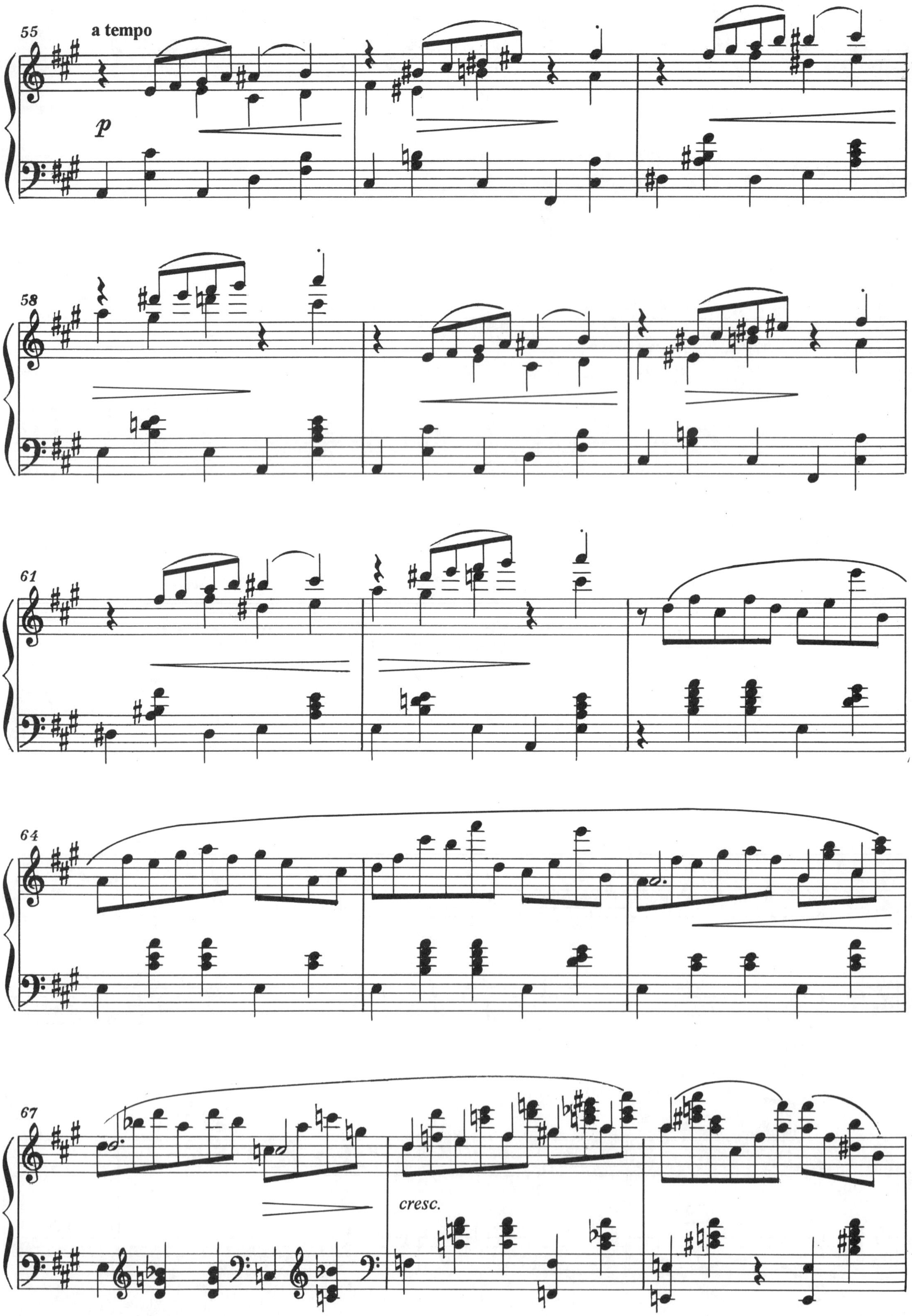
55
a tempo
p
58
61
64
67
cresc.

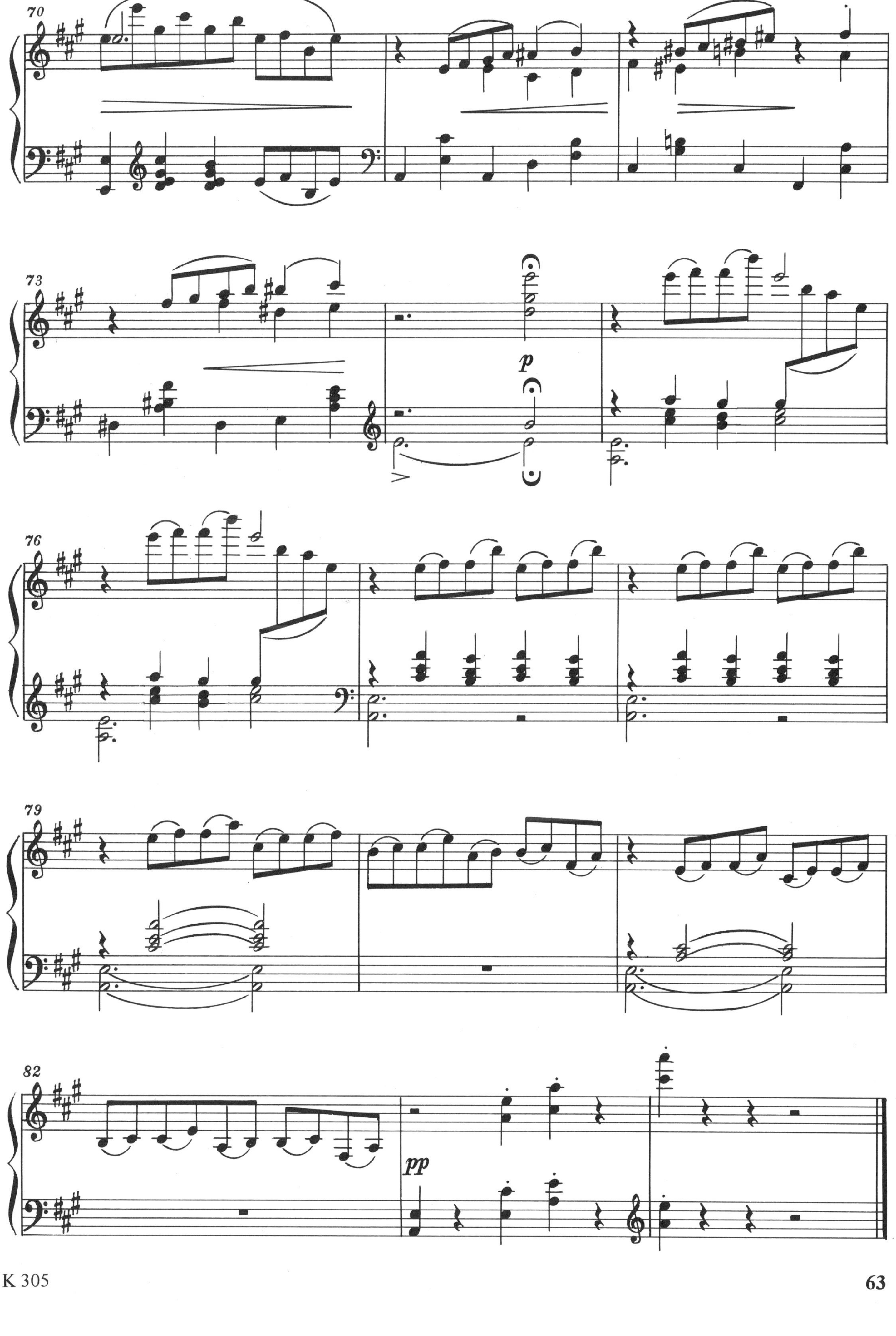
70
73
p
76
79
82
pp

Три багатели Trois Bagatelles
Посвящается Евгении Толкачевой

Op.53.
1903

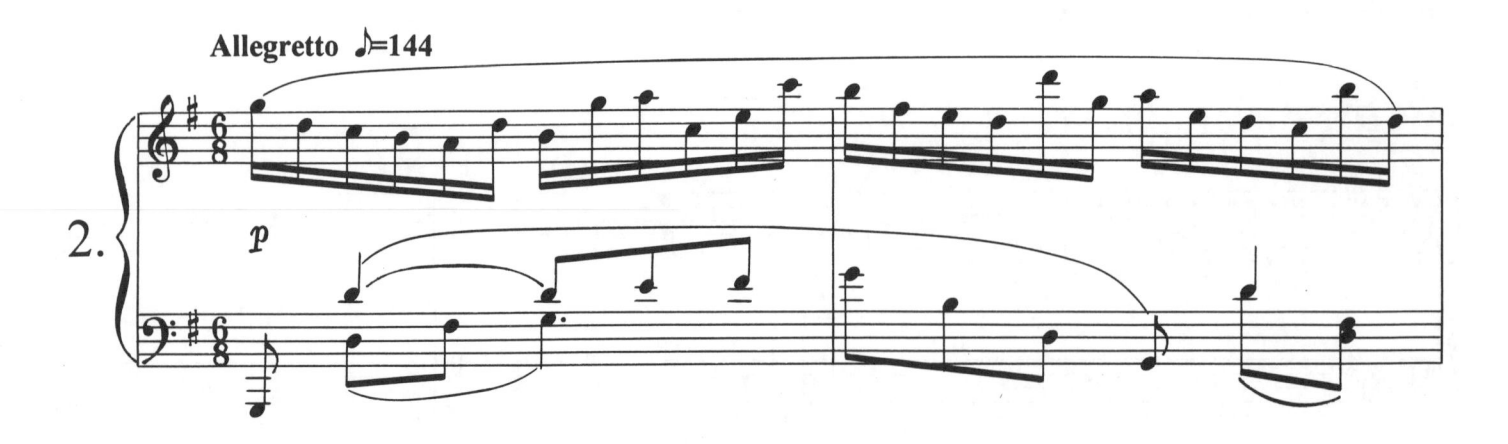

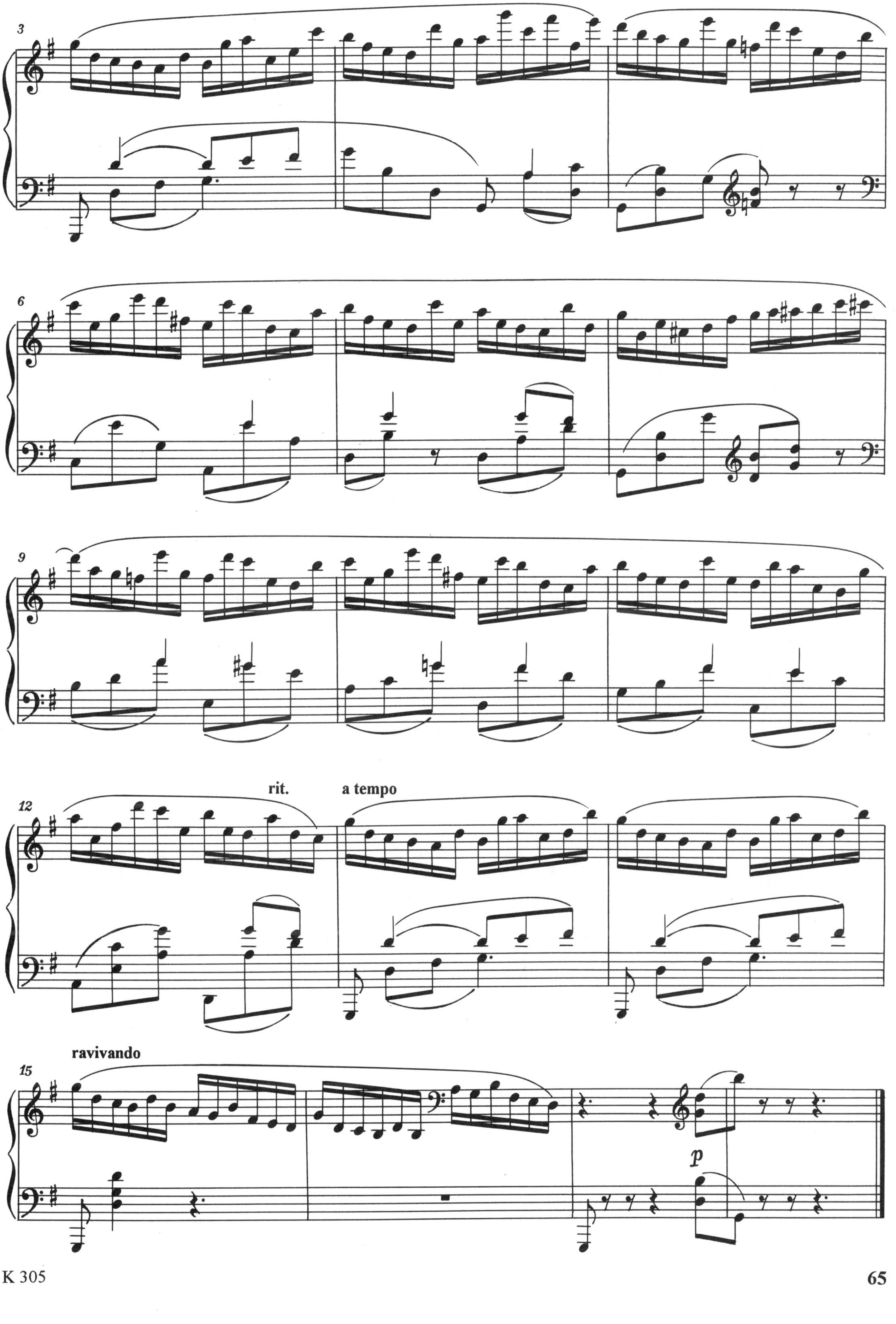
3
6
9
12
rit.
a tempo
15
ravivando
p

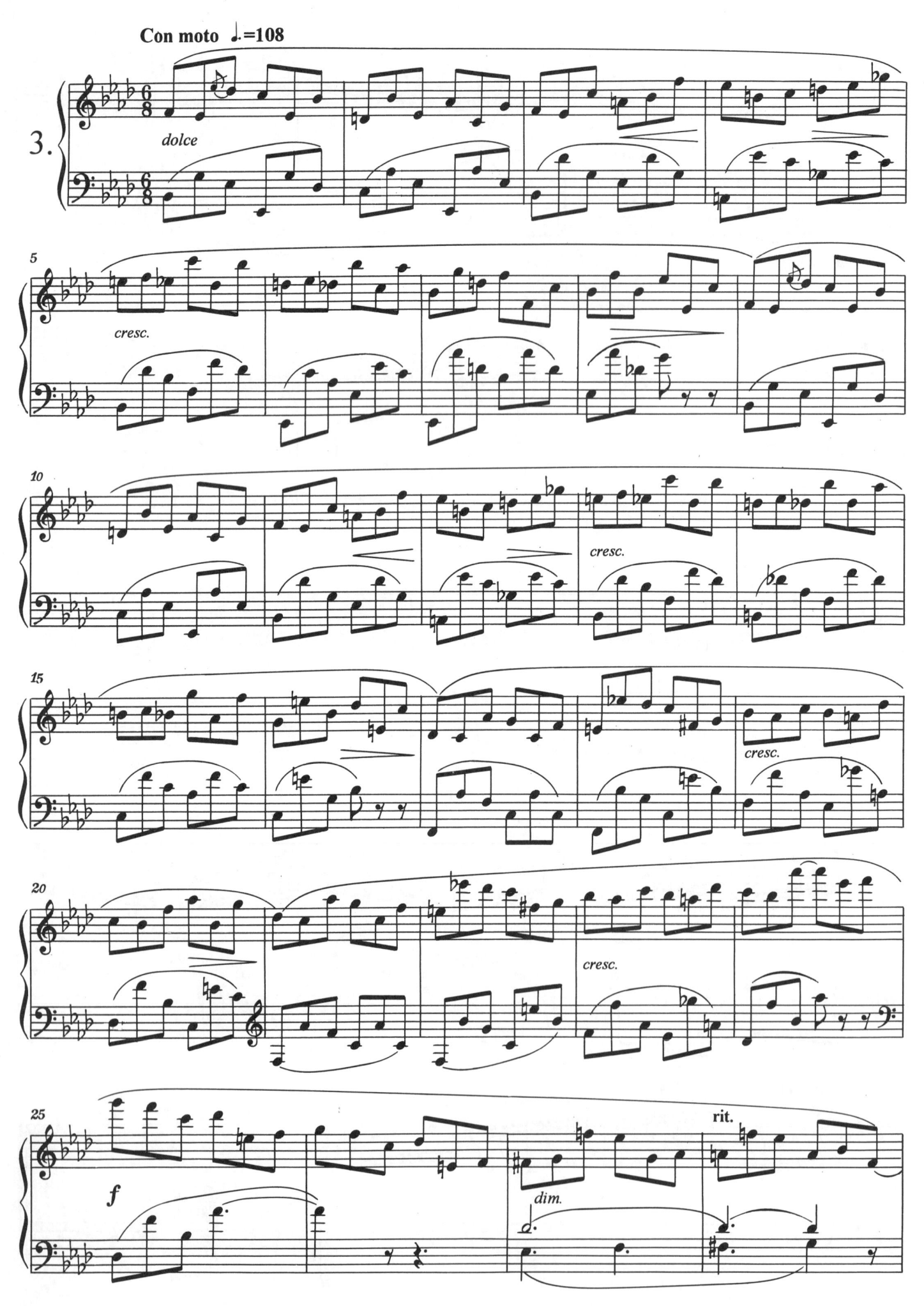
Con moto ♩.=108
3.
dolce
cresc.
cresc.
cresc.
cresc.
f
dim.
rit.

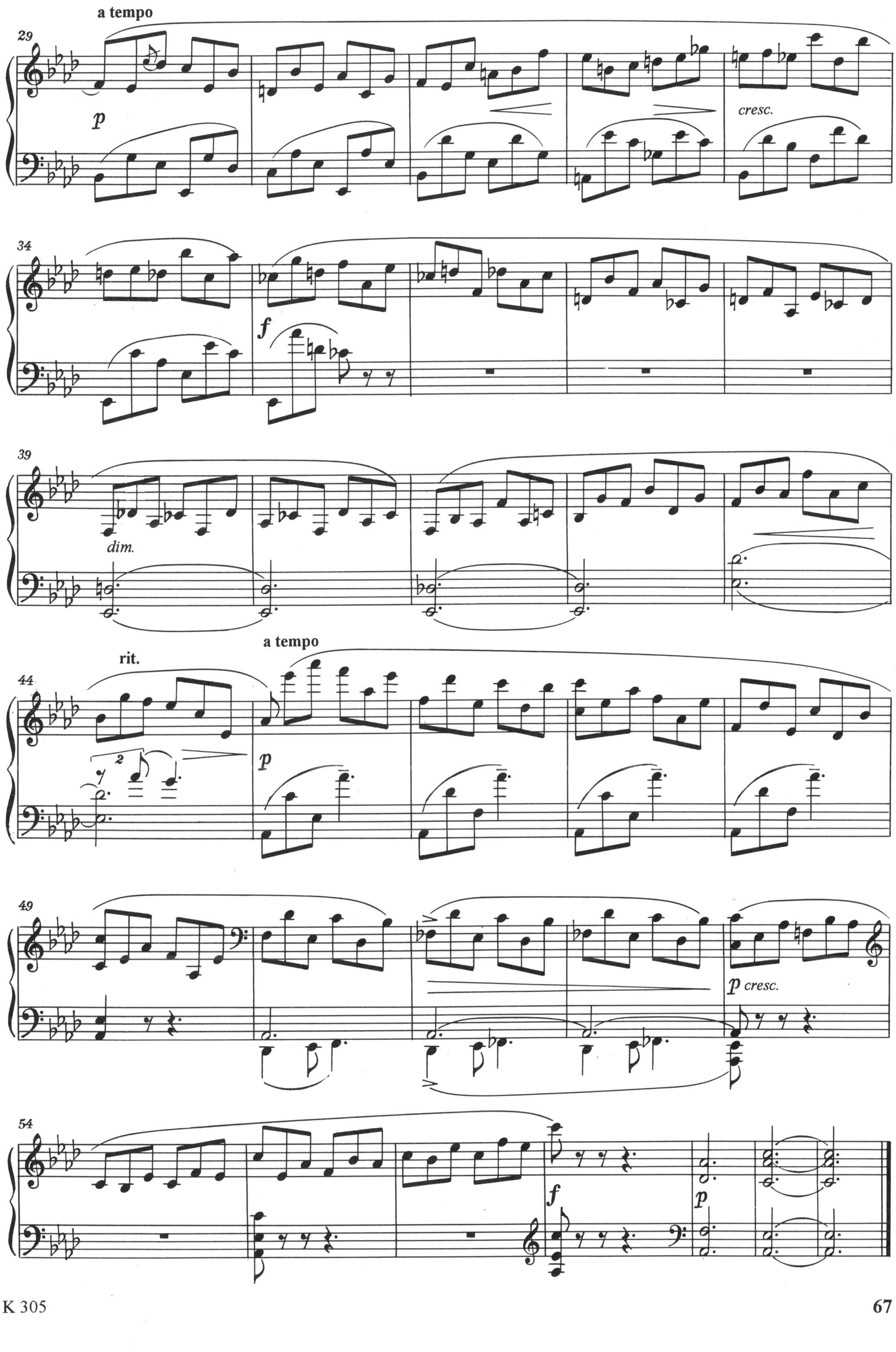
a tempo
29
p
cresc.
34
f
39
dim.
rit.
44
a tempo
p
49
p cresc.
54
f
p

ТРИ ПЬЕСЫ   TROIS MORCEAUX

Op. 57.
1900-1905

Прелюдия   Prélude

A Mademoiselle Marie Tolcatchoff

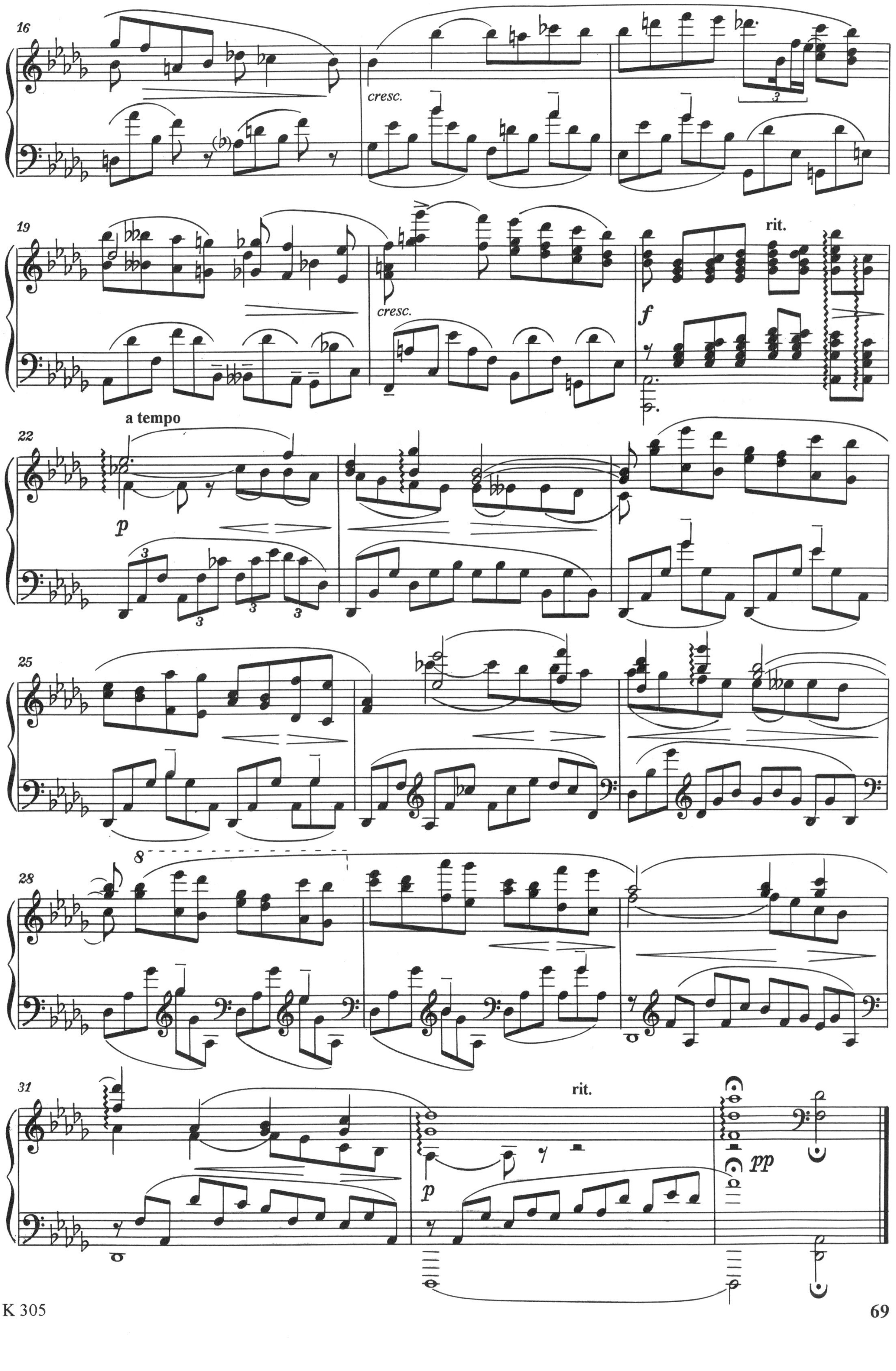
16
cresc.
19
cresc.
rit.
f
a tempo
22
p
25
28
8
31
rit.
p
pp

Вальс   Valse
A Madame Julie Karpinsky

K 305

53
Commodo
accelerando
Allegretto
59
accelerando
65
a tempo
p
cresc.
rit.
a tempo
p
70
cresc.
75
dim.
p
p

Мазурка / Mazurka

A Monsieur Alexandre Karpinsky

ЧЕТЫРЕ ПЬЕСЫ   QUATRE MORCEAUX

Dédié à N. Korsakevitch

Op. 64.
1909-1910

Гримаса   Grimace
Grimace – Grimasse

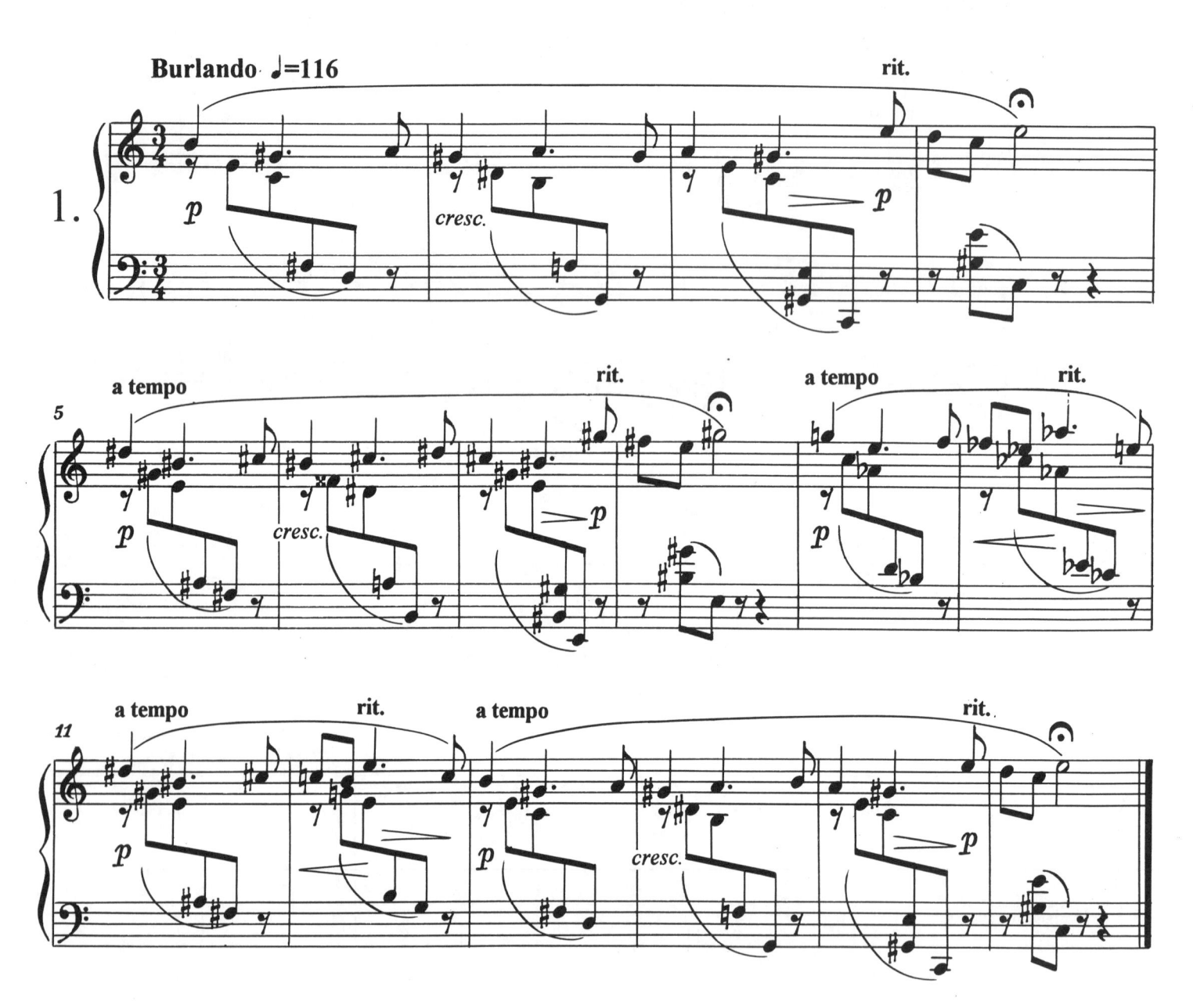

Сумрак   Ténèbres
Twilight – Halbdunkel

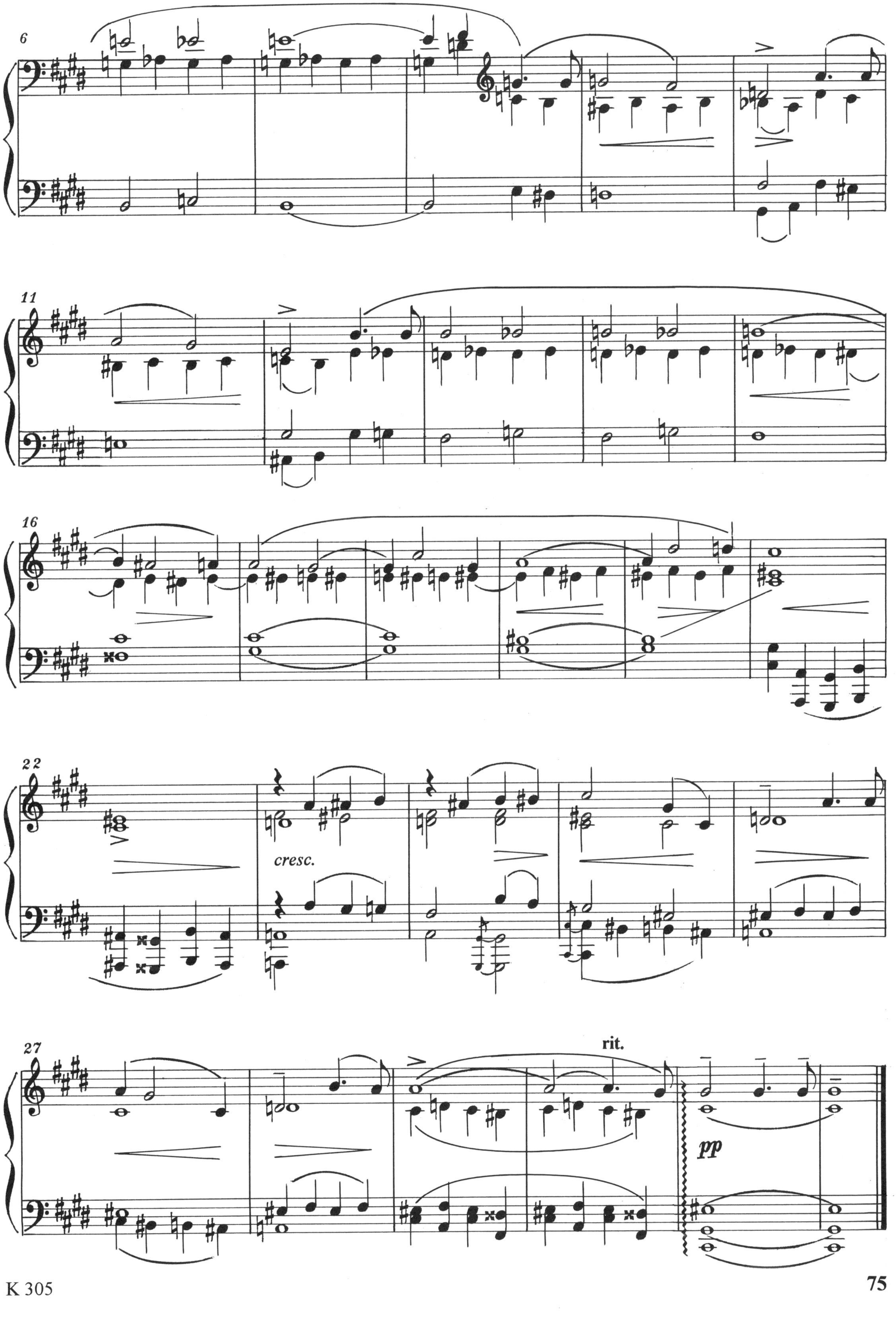
6
11
16
22
cresc.
27
rit.
pp

Искушение Tentation
Temptation – Versuchung

25
p cresc.
dim.
p cresc.
31
dim.
p cresc.
rit.
Tempo I
37
p
accelerando
cresc.
legato
dim.
44
rit.
a tempo
cresc.
f
51
p
rit.
mf
p
pp

Воспоминание   Réminiscence

Reminiscence – Erinnerung

APPENDIX

Шествие / The Procession

М.П.Беляеву

1889

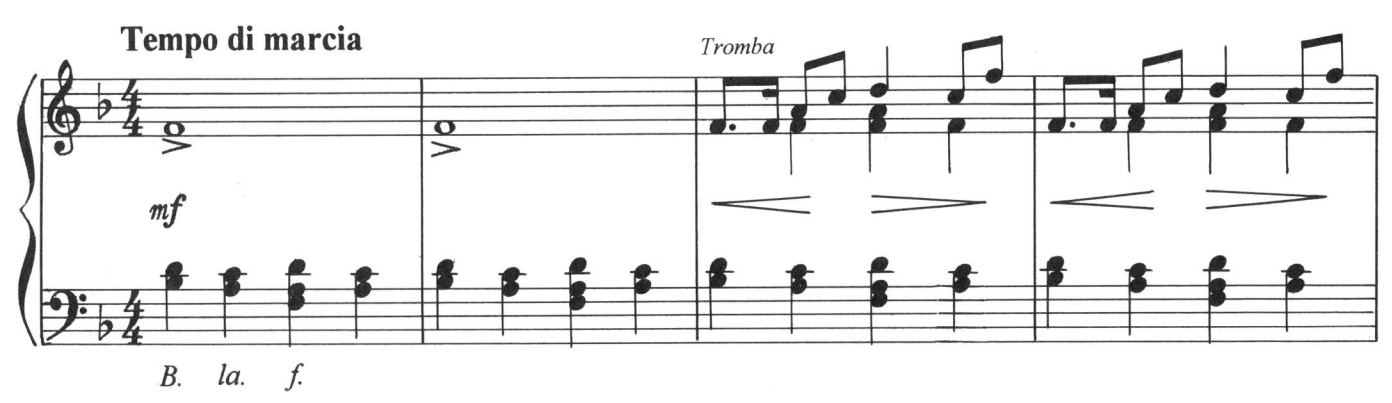

27-го марта 1889 г.

Прелюдия-пастораль

Prélude-pastorale

1894

la melodia ben marcato

Сарабанда   Sarabande

1895

Прелюдия Prélude

Милой Вале

1897

Con moto

La – do – f(a)

3 февраля 1897 г.

Вариации на русскую тему
Variations sur un thème russe

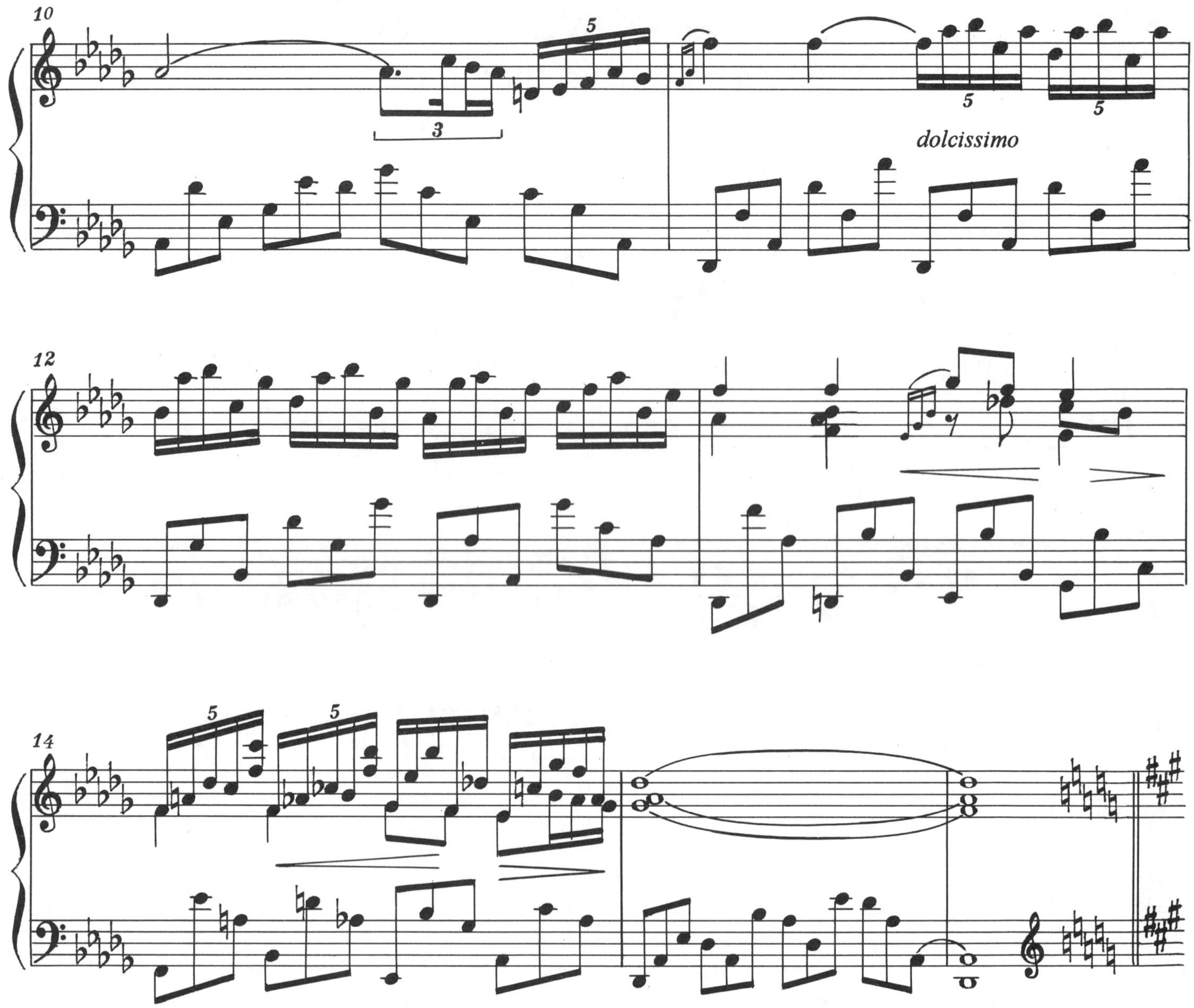

Var. VII

Con moto

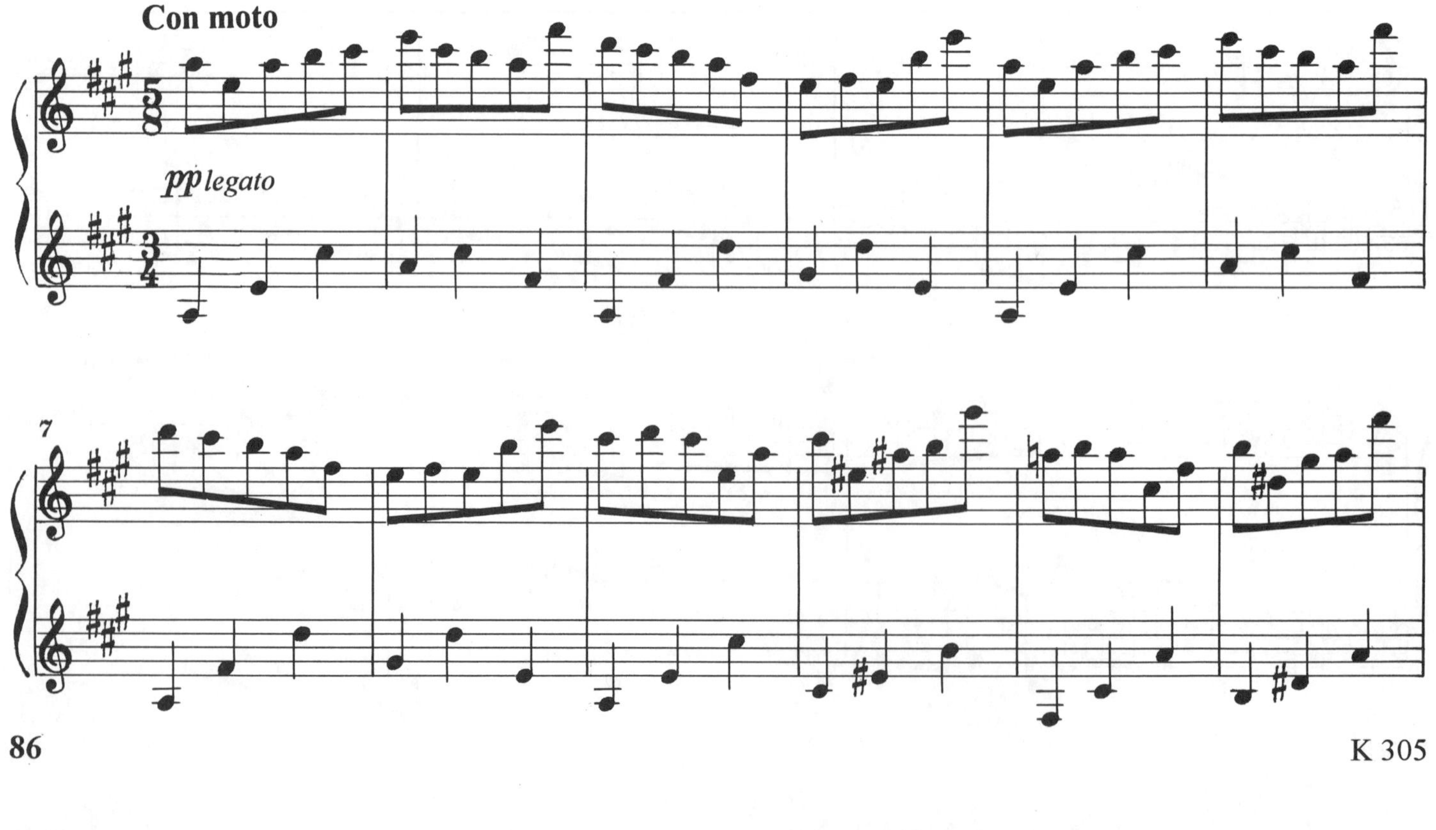

11 декабря 1899 г.

Танец комара / Danse de Moustique

Dance of the Mosquito – Mückentanz

(русская песня)   (chanson russe)

Посвящается Нае Городецкой

1911

Фуга на тему «Ля – До – Фа»
Fugue on the Theme "La – Do – Fa"

1913

30 декабря 1913 г.

12 канонов на один cantus firmus
12 canons on a cantus firmus

Посвящается моему другу Владимиру Александровичу Авдееву

1914

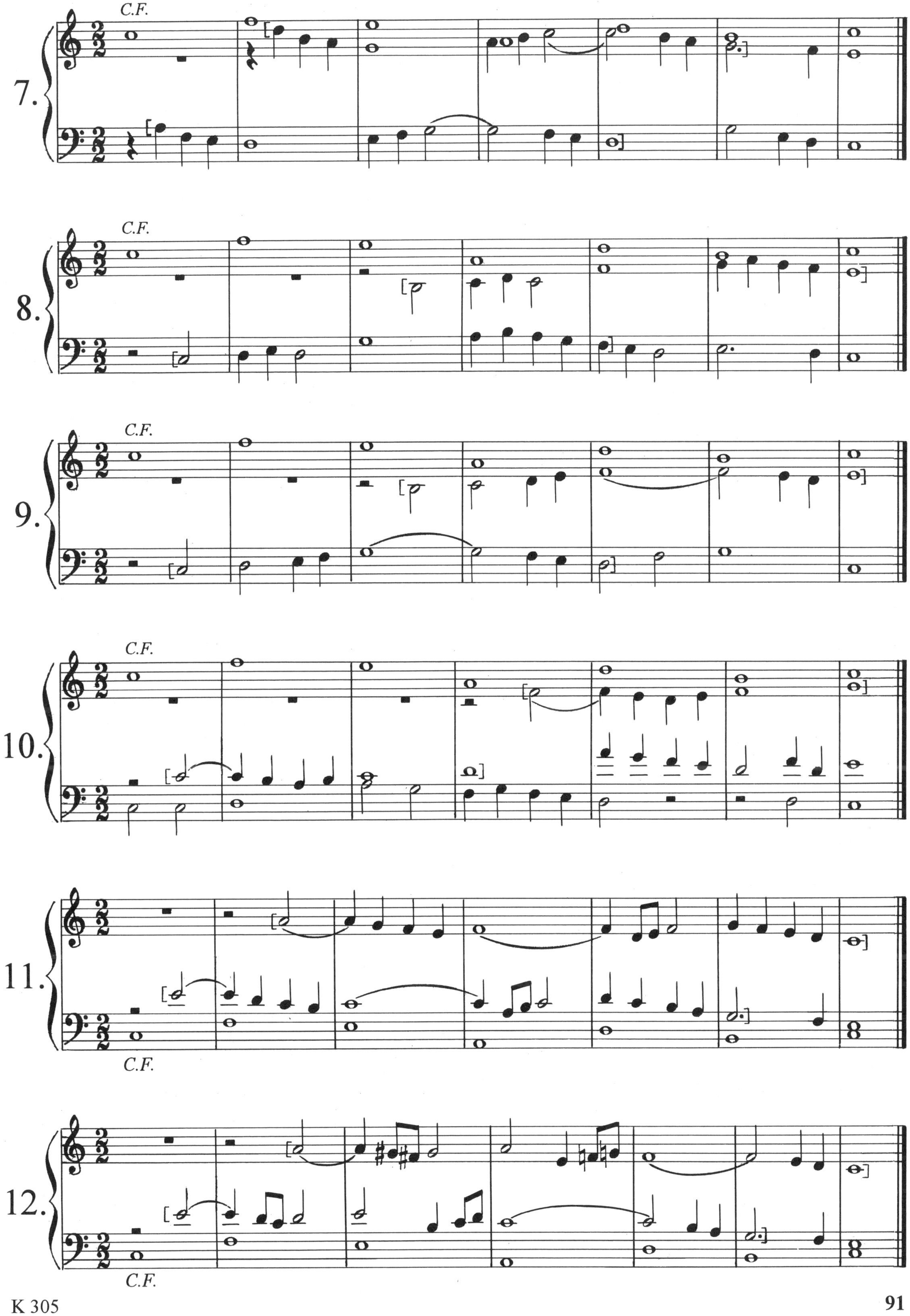
C.F.
7.
C.F.
8.
C.F.
9.
C.F.
10.
11.
C.F.
12.
C.F.

Notes

The present edition contains complete works for piano by A.K.Lyadov in 4 volumes. The works are arranged in chronological order. In the fourth volume are published compositions by Lyadov written in 1896 – 1914. The present edition is based on the autograph manuscript and/or first edition(s) of the works. Other early editions have also been consulted, whenever justified. Evident slips of pen and printing errors have been tacitly corrected. Editorial additions reduced to a minimum appear in square brackets. The composer's peculiarities of notation and original fingering are maintained throughout. All dates are in the Old style.

Deux Fugues op. 41
Autograph: RNL, estate 449, No. 9.
First edition: M. Belyayev (Leipzig, 1897).

Fugue No. 1
Page 5, bar 1, in the first and following editions the *p* indication is missing.
Fugue No. 2
Page 9, bar 1, in the first and following editions the *p* indication is missing.

Deux Préludes et Mazurka op. 42
Autograph: SCMMC, estate 65, No. 7.
First edition: M. Belyayev (Leipzig, 1898).

Barcarolle op. 44
Autograph: RNL, estate 449, No. 6.
First edition: M. Belyayev (Leipzig, 1898).
Page 19, bar 1, no tempo marking found in the autograph.
First edition followed here.

Quatre Préludes op. 46
Autograph: RNL, estate 449, No. 21.
First edition: M. Belyayev (Leipzig, 1899).
Prélude No. 3
Page 27, bar 3, upper staff, the autograph has *c sharp* – instead of *c natural*.
First edition followed here.

Étude et Canzonetta op. 48
The autograph is lost.
First edition: M. Belyayev (Leipzig, 1899).

Variations sur un thème populaire polonais op. 51
Autograph: RNL, estate 449, No. 7.
First edition: M. Belyayev (Leipzig, 1901).

Var. VI, page 45, bar 26, lower stave, the first and following editions have:
The autograph followed here.
Var. VII, page 47, bar 64, the *attacca* indication is missing in the autograph.
First edition followed here.
Var. IX, page 49, bars 9-10 and 25-26, lower stave, tenuto markings from the autograph.
Var. X, page 51, bar 50, lower stave, in the first and following editions the slur is missing.
The autograph followed here.
Coda, page 52, bars 16-17, in the autograph the marking 2/4 is not indicated.

Trois Morceaux de ballet op. 52
Autograph: St. Petersburg Conservatoire, Manuscript department, No. 1706.
First edition: M. Belyayev (Leipzig, 1901).

No. 1
Page 55, bars 51-55, lower stave, the autograph has:

First edition followed here.
Page 56, bars 87 and 91, the indications *più mosso* and *a tempo* not found in the autograph.
Page 56, bars 92-98, lower stave, the autograph has:

First edition followed here.
No. 2
Page 57, no tempo marking found in the autograph.
First edition followed here.
Page 57, bar 31, lower stave, the accent before *g* is not found in the autograph.
First edition followed here.
No. 3
Page 62, bar 69, upper stave, slurs according to the first and following editions:

The autograph followed here.

Trois Bagatelles op. 53
Autograph: St. Petersburg Conservatoire, Manuscript department, No. 1705.
First edition: M. Belyayev (Leipzig, 1903).

Bagatelle No. 3
Page 66, bar 1, no tempo marking found in the autograph.
First edition followed here.

Trois Morceaux op. 57
The autograph is lost.
First edition: M. Belyayev (Leipzig, 1906).

Quatre Morceaux op. 64
The autograph is lost.
First edition: M. Belyayev (Leipzig, 1910).

APPENDIX

The Procession (1889)
The first autograph: RNL, estate 362, list 2, No. 47. The second autograph (identical to the first): RNL, estate 449, No. 22.
First edition followed here.

Prélude-pastorale (1894)
Autograph: SCMMC, estate 65, No.9.
First edition: W. Bessel & Co. St. Petersburg, 1894)

Sarabande (1895)
Autograph: RNL, estate 449, No. 18.
First edition: M. Belyayev (Leipzig, 1895).
'Sarabande' is an item of the set *Three Pieces for String Quartet* composed in 1895 and later arranged for the piano by the composer.

Prélude (1897)
Autograph: Pushkin's House, estate III, list 1, No. 1420 (pages 1-2).
First edition: Kompozitor (St. Petersburg, 1995), in: *Easy Pieces for Piano*, Volume III.
This piece is the first version of the Prelude op. 46, No. 3, published two years later.

Variations sur un thème russe (1899)
Autograph: RNL, estate 1022, No. 2.
First edition: M. Belyayev (Leipzig, 1900).
Variations was composed by N. Rimsky-Korsakov, A. Winkler, F. Blumenfeld, N. Sokolov, J. Witol, A. Lyadov and A. Glazunov. The theme of these variations was the song 'A little Boy' from the *Collection of Russian Folk Songs* by N. Abramychev. Published here are Lyadov's harmonisation of the Theme and the two variations (VI and VII) he composed for this collection.
Thème, page 85, bar 1, no tempo marking found in the autograph.
First edition followed here.

Danse de Moustique (1911)
Autograph: SCMMC, estate 336, No. 41.
First edition: the magazine *Galchyonok*, 1911, No. 2 (St.Petersburg).

Fugue on the Theme "La – Do – Fa" (1913)
The autograph is lost.
First edition: *Russian Musical Newspaper*, 1916, No. 11, in the article 'Letters from A. K. Lyadov to A. V. Ossovsky' (facsimile).

12 canons on a cantus firmus (1914)
The autograph is lost.
First edition: M. Belyayev (Moscow, 1914).

ABBREVIATIONS:

1. CWP   A. Lyadov, Complete works for piano (MUZGIZ, 1947, edited by P. Lamm, L. Oborin, K. Igumnov)
2. IRLRAS   Institute of Russian Literature, Russian Academy of Science (Pushkin's House, St. Petersburg)
3. RNL   Russian National Library (St. Petersburg)
4. SCMMC   State Central Museum of Musical Culture (Moscow)

Anatoly Konstantinovich Lyadov was born on May 11, 1855 in St. Petersburg. His grandfather Nikolay was a conductor of the St. Petersburg Philharmonic, his father Konstantin worked at first as a violinist and from 1850 to 1868 as a conductor of the Mariynsky Theatre in St. Petersburg. Konstantin Lyadov was very talented, but his disordered lifestyle did not allow him to develop his talent. One of his relatives, Varvara Andreyevna Antipova, gave young Anatoly his first piano lessons. As a child Anatoly had a very good voice, but later in his mature years he never sang – he preferred instead to whistle and did it with the virtuosity of a good flutist. In 1870 Lyadov entered the St. Petersburg Conservatory, where he studied piano with Professor Kross, special theory, harmony, counterpoint and fugue with Professor Johansen and composition with Professor Nikolay Rimsky-Korsakov. In 1878 Lyadov graduated from the Conservatory with a Small Silver Medal and was invited to be an assistant teacher of elementary classes for theory, later becoming professor at this institution, teaching special classes of harmony and composition. He also held a similar position in the Imperial Court Chapel. Together with Balakirev and Lyapunov he was commissioned by the Imperial Geographical Society to conduct research of the folksongs in various districts.

Lyadov composed many of his best pieces for piano. His compositions are delicate and graceful, and the influence of Chopin is clearly evident in these pieces. At the same time their distinctively Russian colouring and humorous character saves his music from the reproach of servile imitation. Some of Lyadov's piano pieces have been orchestrated and used for ballets in the repertoire of the Dyaghilev company in his "Russian Seasons" in Paris. (The ballet "Russian Fairy Tales", based on the "Eight Russian Folksongs" for orchestra, was used together with numerous orchestrated piano pieces).

Lyadov was often reproached with indolence by his friends, who thought so highly of his gift that they wished to see it used in large-scale works, but Lyadov knew his limits and preferred to work effectively within them, and perhaps his busy life as a teacher also prevented his undertaking large compositions and completing the ballet he had began. He made three attempts to compose an opera and in 1877 began a string quartet. Nevertheless, his orchestral works, though not extensive, are beautifully finished and scored with a highest mastery.

A very special place in Lyadov's life belongs to Mitrofan Petrovich Belyayev, a very rich timber merchant, a famous lover of music and patron of arts. Belyayev in 1884 had founded a music publishing house in Leipzig in order to promote new compositions of Russian composers. In 1885 he had founded the series of Russian Symphonic Concerts in St. Petersburg and in 1891 the series of Russian Quartet Nights. For the first time Belyayev met Lyadov at one of the concerts, where Lyadov performed as a conductor. Belyayev valued Lyadov not only as a talented musician and composer, but also as a man devoted to his profession with a very modest attitude to his own compositions. Belyayev had decided that it was his sacred duty to help Lyadov in his struggle with the difficulties of practical life. This relationship served as an important moral support for Lyadov in the difficulties of life. When Belyayev was told that Lyadov was very lazy and put very little time into his composing, he tried to demand that Lyadov "compose and compose more". Belyayev received a letter from Lyadov: "... I'm very sorry that you see only one side of my character – "the good pal" – but I have other sides too. I will never tolerate violence or authority, even if it comes out of love or friendship... I will terminate any relationships immediately if they become uncomfortable for me...".

The first composition by Lyadov published by Belyayev in 1888 was the "Mazurka for Orchestra". It was performed on 5 December 1887 in Belyayev's Russian Symphonic Concerts under the baton of Rimsky-Korsakov.

The aesthetic position of Lyadov was very unusual for the Russian composers, writers and artists. In his letter to N. Korsakevich (5 January 1905) he wrote: "I may live comfortably without Tolstoi – I don't need him. He died for me long ago: since he started writing "for people" and becoming "a useful artist"... He is a man of "guts", not a man of spirit. By his opinion God and the arts ought to be useful. He is my enemy from head to heels. He is the same as Gorky. I am disgusted by Tolstoi and Gorky, by their "street" success and common philosophy. They have minds of "grass" not minds of "rose". These men help mankind to commit the greatest crime of the world – to level everybody". Later, about 1910 Lyadov was inspired by the philosophy of Nietzsche. In Nietzsche's works Lyadov found the support for his aspiration to individual freedom, based on his contempt of the masses. In the letter to O. Korsakevich (19 December 1911) Lyadov wrote: "If you would like to become free – destroy all inherited family customs and thoughts in yourself, become intellectually naked – and create yourself from the beginning". The only Russian writer whom Lyadov adored till the end of his life was Pushkin. "O Pushkin, Pushkin! Eternal, radiant, free artist – from head to heels! Only before him shall I kneel" (letter to N. Korsakevich, 30 July 1907). "I'm a "free bird". The word "must" will never force me to do anything. My desire is my law. Probably (or certainly) it's bad – but it's my nature" (from Lyadov's diaries, 29 April 1907).

Anatoly Konstantinovich Lyadov died of pneumonia on 28 August 1914 in Polynovka.

KÖNEMANN MUSIC BUDAPEST
November 2000

PÄDAGOGISCHE AUSGABEN
für Klavier
PEDAGOGICAL EDITIONS
for piano

PIANO STEP BY STEP

Alte Tänze – *Early Dances*
Einführung in das polyphone Spiel – *Introduction to Polyphonic Playing*
Erste Konzertstücke – *First Concert Pieces* I–II–III–IV
Etüden
Sonatinen I–II–III
Vierhändige Klaviermusik – *Works for Piano Duet* I–II–III

J. S. Bach: 37 Piano Pieces
L. van Beethoven: 47 Piano Pieces
E. Grieg: 37 Piano Pieces
J. Haydn: 23 Piano Pieces
W. A. Mozart: 44 Piano Pieces

IN VORBEREITUNG – *IN PREPARATION*
Cornelius Gurlitt: 56 Piano Pieces
Die Bach Söhne – *The Bach' Sons*

FAVOURITE PIANO STUDIES

Carl Czerny:
100 Übungsstücke – *100 Exercises,* Op. 139
Die Schule der Geläufigkeit – *School of Velocity,* Op. 299
Kunst der Fingerfertigkeit – *The Art of Finger Dexterity,* Op. 740 I–II

IN VORBEREITUNG – *IN PREPARATION*
160 kurze Übungen – *160 Little Exercises*

Pekka Vapaavuori–Hannele Hynninen
Der Barockpianist – *The Baroque Pianist*

IN VORBEREITUNG – *IN PREPARATION*
Grundschule für Klavier – *Elementary Piano School* I–IV

FAVOURITES for Piano

Favourite Ballet Classics I–II (Tchaikovsky)
Favourite Opera Classics I–II (Mozart)
Favourite Opera Classics III–IV (Verdi)
Favourite Opera Classics V–VI (Italian Composers)
Favourite Piano Classics I–IV
Amazing Grace and Other Popular American Songs
American Classical Songs I–II
Cream of Irish Songs I
John Brown and Other Popular American Songs
Oh, When the Saints Go Marchin' in and Other Popular American Songs
O Sole Mio and Other Popular Italian Songs
Scott Joplin: Ragtimes
Spirituals
Johann Strauss: Walzer
100 deutsche Kinderlieder – *100 German Children's Songs*

IN VORBEREITUNG – *IN PREPARATION*
Cream of Irish Songs II
Italienische Lieder – *Italian Songs* II

KAMMERMUSIK
CHAMBER MUSIC

Cello Meets Piano I–II
Flute Meets Piano I–II
Violin Meets Piano I–II

KLAVIERAUSZÜGE
VOCAL SCORES

Johann Sebastian Bach:
Johannes-Passion
Magnificat
Matthäus-Passion
Weihnachts-Oratorium
Kantaten – *Cantatas*
   Christ lag in Todes Banden
   Ein feste Burg ist unser Gott
   Ich hatte viel Bekümmernis
   Ich will den Kreuzstab gerne tragen
   Wachet auf, ruft uns die Stimme
   Weinen, Klagen, Sorgen, Zagen

IN VORBEREITUNG – *IN PREPARATION*
Bauernkantate
Kaffekantate

Georg Friedrich Händel:
Der Messias – *The Messiah*

Joseph Haydn: Nelson Messe

Wolfgang Amadeus Mozart: Requiem

Giovanni Battista Pergolesi:
Stabat Mater

GITARRE – GUITAR

Mauro Giuliani:
Variationen
Luis Milán:
El Maestro (1536) I–II
Fernando Sor–Matteo Carcassi:
Klassische Etüden – *Classical Studies*
Francisco Tárrega:
Originalkompositionen – *Original Compositions*

© 2000 for this edition by Könemann Music Budapest Kft.
H–1093 Budapest, Közraktár utca 10.

K 305

Distributed worldwide by Könemann Verlagsgesellschaft mbH,
Bonner Str. 126. D–50968 Köln

Responsible co-editor: Vladimir Ryabov
Production: Detlev Schaper
Cover design: Peter Feierabend
Technical editor: Dezső Varga
Engraved in Russia

Printed by Kossuth Printing House Co., Budapest
Printed in Hungary

ISBN 963 9155 43 8